Journey
on a Stairwell

WILLIAM GRIMES

NORTH MAIN PRESS

D1070254

Published by North Main Press

First North Main Press Edition, December 2019

Published in the United States of America
ISBN: 978-1-7330312-2-6
Body, Mind & Spirit / Spiritualism 16.01.21

Cover photo by Jeff Grimes
Author photo by Coby Roland

This book is dedicated to my parents, Leonard and Ellen Grimes. Without their unfailing support and hard work, the transition of the residence into my dental office would not have been possible.

Acknowledgments

The author wishes to thank the following for their contributions toward this work; their diligent assistance and tireless efforts helped make this book possible.

Lisa McClure-Donnelly, who turned my scribbles into legible print. Huntington Paranormal Investigations and Research, who did an enormous amount of detective work piecing together the facts about the history of the building and the Wall family. Janet Grimes for her editing skills. Dozens of paranormal groups who helped discover the "others" who inhabited the building. Dr. Thomas Grimes, who used computer magic to make my illustrations printable. All of the people who had the courage to write their experiences in the Ghost Log.

Finally, I want to thank an anonymous medium who found the final piece of the puzzle in the mystery of Lavina Wall.

Contents

Prologue

They're gone now. My time with them has come to an abrupt end. It took me several weeks to realize what had happened—that they had simply passed from our plane of existence. Contact with us became something that, for whatever reason, could no longer be. As in the moment of a chance encounter with a creature in the wild, when we experience a range of emotions involving surprise, wonder, appreciation and, lastly, sadness when they quietly turn away and vanish into their realm with silent, elegant grace. And so it was with them.

This is a story about the hereafter, of time and space, and what we learn when their intersection forms eternity. It was a journey for me; a journey on a stairwell. It was a passage that opened my mind to the reality of the afterlife and the truth of the existence of the soul. On that stairwell, a battle was waged. It was a struggle between good and evil. In that space, the soul of a small girl was taken from a harsh life, held earthbound in a form of purgatory, and at last given a way to find eternal peace.

Not long ago, I stood at the railing and looked down the stairwell, recalling the events that had unfolded there, the people who had helped me learn the truth behind what had happened, and the importance this would eventually have in my life. All this came to me in a moment of quiet solitude as the setting sun cast both rays of amber light and deepening shadows in the upstairs hallway and down into the stairwell. The tranquil scene contrasted completely with the hectic day I had just finished. As I watched the play of light and shadows, I could imagine the spirit realm that occupied that area for so many years. "Good-bye, Livy. I wish you well," was my brief epitaph, understated as it was. Perhaps it was an inadequate summation, considering all the profound experiences so many had encountered within and around that space but, at the time, it seemed appropriate.

1

First Impressions

The duplex numbered 1125 and 1127 Twentieth Street had apparently been known as a haunted house for a considerable amount of time before I bought it. One might ask, "When did all that begin?" Was it haunted before October 29, 1929? That is anyone's guess, but at some time after that date, it did become haunted. That is certain, for on that day, a girl died in the bedroom at the top of the stairs on the north side of the duplex, and her soul remained there.

My first encounter with the house occurred when I was just a kid, wet behind the ears. At the time, I was a grade-schooler and the youngest of four children, with two brothers and one sister. One of my brothers, Tom, was given an assignment by his high school English teacher. It involved a television program; a play that was scheduled to air that week. He and his classmates were to watch the show at home and write a paper about the plot of the play and what they thought of it. I have no recollection of the play, but it was probably one of Shakespeare's tragedies. My mother struck upon a splendid idea. She suggested that Dad should contact Mr. Jim Grass, an old friend of the family, and ask him if we could watch the program on one of his color television sets at his Muntz TV store. That way, the entire family could watch the program in color.

Mr. Grass had often invited Dad to his store to see a show on one of his floor model television sets so that Dad could really appreciate the quality of the new color programs being offered on our three local channels. He had even insisted that Dad should bring along the whole family and we could make an outing of it. Dad could not argue with the logic of the plan, so he set up the date for us to meet Mr. Grass to watch the play on a big screen in living color. At that time, only a limited number of programs were presented in color. The majority of programming was done in black and white. This even included the evening news programs. When the appointed day arrived, Mom and Dad packed us into the family car, a Kaiser, and off to the Muntz TV store we went.

The store occupied one half of the first floor of a brick building that still stands to this day on the corner of Twentieth Street and Charleston Avenue. To the left of Muntz TV, the other half of the first floor was a grocery called Boster's. The twin first floor business fronts had their entrances in the center of each half. The entrances were flanked on each side by large plate glass windows. The two central doors were recessed a bit so that smaller windows, set at slight angles to the larger windows, formed alcoves in which one could stand and view items for sale. Late-nineteenth-century-styled wood panels set off the two fronts above and below the array of windows and doors, stretching across the entire front of the first floor. On the second floor were apartments that had a side entrance onto Charleston Avenue.

We arrived early, but when we pulled to the front of the building, the sun had already set. It was dark. Instead of waiting in the car for Mr. Grass to arrive, I got out and went over to the left side window of the store. A large black and gold banner with gold tassels hanging down each side proudly proclaimed the brand of televisions that were sold there—at Muntz TV. Beneath this heraldic banner sat proudly on a raised and spotlighted platform a large floor model in blond oak. It seemed to be offering an invitation to step inside. Beyond this magnificent piece of engineering and cabinetry, I could see in the half-lit showroom other equally impressive sets arranged at odd angles around the area like so many caskets in a mortuary. We had an uncle by marriage who was a mortician, so even as a child I was very familiar with that darker part of human existence. Seeing caskets with dead people in them was nothing new to the four of us children, since we visited the mortuary nearly every time we saw our cousins. (The place had a naturally magnetic draw for inquisitive youngsters like us.) So, in my imagination, the large wooden cabinets of the sets morphed into caskets where death resided in elegant repose. These trips into my vivid imagination were seldom shared with others. They were created by me for me. I never felt any need to share, so I never told anyone about this time spent out of the car looking into the showroom of Muntz TV. As I stood there, the floor models returned to being just that—floor model televisions. My imagination had concluded its odd reverie, and I returned to the reality of the scene at hand.

It was a cold, damp night. Rain had been falling off and on all through the day, so when the sun set, it did so behind gray clouds that formed an unbroken pearly veil that turned into a black dome of immeasurable density. It revealed nothing but a starless, moonless abyss.

I wondered if Mr. Grass would try to get Dad to buy one of those huge sets. I was sure we could afford none of them. My parents were facing college expenses soon in an unbroken cadence of the four of us, as we became high school graduates and college applicants. My parents were always looking toward that time, and for them our educations were far more important than a floor model television. Compared to these wooden limousines, our set at home was like a tiny newborn offspring. It would look silly sitting on the floor of our living room. Instead, it resided on a television table. This was a recent development in the jargon of home furnishings. This new piece of furniture found its way into the majority of homes at that time since not that many homeowners could afford the bigger sets, let alone the new color ones. For our television table, Tom made an outstanding example in woodworking shop at Huntington East High School. It was made of beautiful clear-grained mahogany with turned legs. Stained a deep red, it was a perfect companion to our set. He still has this table in his home, except that now the legs are shorter, having been cut down to a height more commensurate to that of a bedside table. Televisions were placed on these special tables with longer legs than any other table in a home. The experts of the day on the subject of television viewing strongly advised their public that the optimal height of a television screen should be not less than forty-two inches from the floor. Damage to the eyes could result from an improper viewing angle. Then out came the floor models with their screens located much lower. The experts came out with a new admonishment. Screens must be at the height at which one would read a book while sitting in a comfortable chair. And with this new edict, the television tables disappeared from furniture stores and households, to be forgotten, along with slate blackboards in public schools.

I turned away from the luxurious televisions and the store front and strolled along the building to its inner corner and glanced down the space between the store and the house next door. Rain glazed the surface of the scene with an unfriendly sparkle of cold light caused by the splashes of the soft rain droplets that set fairylike movement in the dark shadows of bricks, pavement, and a rusted chain-link fence that bordered two identical houses located next to the building where Muntz TV roosted like a squawky tropical bird. Compared to Muntz, the two houses presented a scene of quiet gloom.

At once, my attention was fixed on the house nearest to where I was standing. It was as if that house had stepped suddenly out of the gloomy mist and stood there glaring down at me, without even a hint of welcome. A span of dark-green awning divided the face of the thing into its upper floors and those below, but they were hidden under the dark brow of that awning and the shadowy gloom of the wet porch beneath it. The awning was the only difference between the two houses, but what a difference it made. Or was there more to it than just that? As I studied the house, I began to feel a sadness emanating from it. Then I felt something in addition to the sadness. It was mixed with something like a warning. I felt a bit afraid of it. I wondered why I felt that way as I looked at the house. It struck me as something that I should avoid, something to back away from, and so I did. I went to the curb where our Kaiser was parked and climbed back onto the large couch seat with my siblings, saying nothing. As I sat there, my thoughts returned to the sensation I had felt as I looked at the strange house with the dark-green awning. In this case, I could not say that my imagination had created a monster of some sort out of large white house. No, this was not my imagination. This time, it was something different. But what? I glanced through the rain-distorted window. There it was again. It seemed to look back with its darkened windows that glared at me like the eye sockets of a huge skull.

What if I had said anything of what I was feeling about that house? I knew my brothers would have twisted such observations and reactions into a comedy routine, so I would not even consider telling them what I had discovered there. My brother Jim was the family comedian par excellence. At the dinner table he would use the slightest misstep any of us made in action or conversation and turn it into an impromptu comedic monologue that would have all of the rest of us laughing to the point of tears. I remember my mother on so many of those occasions wiping tears from her eyes with her napkin as she giggled, recounting what Jim had just said. I thought this occasion, should I reveal the experience, would provide grist for a similar display of his humoresque genius. No, it was best to keep quiet.

Mr. Grass pulled up behind our car, and we all got out of the Kaiser and went inside to watch our program on the big Muntz TV in magnificent color. Mr. Grass did not assail Dad with any pressure to buy one of the sets. Instead, he sat with us in an arc of chairs facing the big screen, drinking coffee and eating the peanut butter cookies that Mom had brought for the occasion. The eerie feeling that I had experienced while looking at the foreboding house next door was forgotten. At least for the time being.

Figure 1: The duplex 1125 and 1127 Twentieth Street. The building to the left with the sign, "Children Evangelism Fellowship" is a mission that had previously been. Muntz TV.

2

Ghosts Vanish in the Sunlight, Don't They?

Almost twenty years later, early in September of 1973, I was standing at that same spot on Twentieth Street near the inner corner of the same red-brick building, looking at the same white house with clapboard siding and that same dark-green awning. Only on this occasion there was the warm sunshine of a bright midday, and I was considering buying the house. As before, my parents were there, too, but gone was the Kaiser. Gone was the store where Mr. Grass sold Muntz television sets. Gone, also, was the twin clapboard house that stood to the right of the house I was now intending to buy. I was now a dentist looking for a place to establish my practice. In place of that house was now a modern building that was the new location of Gladwell Pharmacy that a pharmacist, Mr. Dozier, had built after tearing down the clapboard house. This new building and the red-brick building on the corner were built out, even with each other, almost to the sidewalk. This caused the house between them to be set back even to a greater degree than when the two houses stood together and only the red brick was set out. For me, this was a good thing because it would allow me to build an addition out even with the two buildings on either side without having to obtain a variance from the city government. My first-floor plan would be greatly increased.

In place of Muntz TV, there was a Christian outreach child day care center. Gone was the gaudy black and gold banner with its gold tassels. In place of its proud heraldic proclamation was a plain-blue sign with white letters that announced, without any great pride, the new purpose the location had to offer. The changes to the area I now surveyed, the bright, warm sunlight, and my restless mind toying with a myriad of possibilities, all put the duplex at 1125 and 1127 Twentieth Street in a different perspective than what I had seen on that gloomy night some twenty years before. I wanted to buy it. I needed to put myself into a dental office as quickly as possible because I had a roster of patients who needed my attention. This place fell within my budget and, with luck, could be converted into an office quickly. It would also be located next to a pharmacy. That would open opportunities, especially since Mr. Dozier said he would allow my patients and staff to access my parking lot through his parking lot and would allow us to park on his lot as well. His was far more than he needed. It wrapped all the way around his pharmacy, behind my property, and extended to Charleston Avenue. My patients and staff would have a very large parking area to choose from. This was an important part of the plan to buy the property when I discovered that the bureaucrats at city hall would not consider my application for building permits without a notarized statement from Mr. Dozier stipulating our off-street parking agreement. I had one more important reason to buy this house. I had looked all over town for a home for my practice and this location seemed to be the most practical. I lacked the capital to tear the structure down and build an entirely new one from the ground up, as Mr. Dozier had done with his pharmacy. Instead, I had to remodel, and I would have to watch my expenses. There would be little room for mistakes in planning, and I could afford no major surprises that would result in an increase in the cost. All these things and much more were whirling in my head.

Mr. Dozier was actively talking up the sale. He had, from his side of the equation, some very good reasons to assist me in the decision to buy the place. He was forthright with his motives. He wanted me in the building so that he could rest assured that one weak area of the security of his pharmacy would be nullified by my presence in the building next to his. This was because the two-story house had second-floor windows that were only a short distance from the roof of his pharmacy. One could just about jump from one of those windows onto his roof. Easier still would be the placement of a plank from one of the windows, across the open space, and onto his roof. He told me that he had spent more than one sleepless night thinking about that. The owner of the house had rejected repeated offers by Mr. Dozier to buy the house so that he could tear it down and eliminate the threat those second floors presented. After years of trying, he gave up. Then, property behind the house came up for sale and Mr. Dozier bought it so that parking would be available from Twentieth Street and Charleston Avenue as well. Then, without warning, the owner next door put her house up for sale. Mr. Dozier was now short on cash to buy it, so his plan to put me in it worked well for him. He also developed a plan that would make it attractive for me to send patients into his pharmacy for free toothbrushes. As it turned out, we did this for many years after I opened my office. I also purchased many supplies for the office from him. And so the pharmacy and the dental office developed a longstanding relationship that was mutually beneficial. Mr. Dozier's plan worked out very well.

I knew the transition from duplex rental residence to dental office would be difficult, but I planned to rent out one side of my duplex to another professional, which would help offset costs of construction and, at a later time, the costs of operating the practice would be offset by the rental income. To make this idea work, I needed to build the extension out from the front of the house. With this addition, there would be room enough to make the office work. The porch would be the first victim of demolition to make the extension possible.

Mrs. Bowen, the proprietor of the duplex, stood in her living room without the hint of a gracious little old lady. There were no cups of tea offered, and we were obliged to stand through the entire meeting since she did not offer seats to any of us. We conducted the introductions and details of the sale on our feet. Her cold demeanor, perhaps born out of dealing with renters of unsavory natures, was not improved by our courteous approbations. With a hard look at us, she presented a verbal list of conditions within the sale agreement that she had no intention of backing away from in any form. The owner of 1125 and 1127 Twentieth Street was then finally willing to sell the house.

These conditions were attached to the structure of the house rather than any intangible clauses of a purely legal nature. She wanted to take with her, prior to the completion of the agreement, the large aluminum awning on the front porch, some light fixtures from her side of the duplex, and some faucets and sinks. We cheerfully agreed that those items would not present any problems for us and that she was welcome to have them removed prior to our taking over the place. We had not been planning to retain any of the items she mentioned anyway. I noticed that this gratuity did not dent her fixed expression in any way. The meeting was a difficult and awkward experience. Mr. Dozier made the introductions and presented our side of the sale since she knew him, and she had never seen either my father or me before. My father was there because he was my cosigner for the loan. I had not established a credit line of sufficient stature to approach the gods of banking with a supplication of such magnitude. It was a very stiff and formal hostess who opened the door and wished us an icy good-bye. I do not recall being in the place with Mrs. Bowen any time after that one instance. I really didn't want to anyway. Dad wondered if the presence of Mr. Dozier had made some difference in her behavior. We all talked about it as one strange meeting. Mr. Dozier noted that every time he had dealings with her, she had acted that way. I thought there was more to it than that. I had no idea what it might have been, but she seemed to have something on her mind that had nothing to do with the three of us.

It was odd, looking back on that time, that I chose to set up my office in the duplex side that Mrs. Bowen had rented out. I never once considered using the side she lived in, in spite of the fact that she took far better care of her side than she did of the rental side. What drew me to that side even before having entered it? Was some mystical appeal emanating from within? Before long, the duplex of 1125 and 1127 would become just 1125, and the number 1127, Mrs. Bowen's side, would be dropped as the formal address. As it turned out, that address may well have been absent from the ghost stories that were told about the place. And so, the north side, 1125, may have been the stage of verbal dramas told on porches during languid summer nights and in parlors on long cold winter evenings. Were the ghosts in 1125 the reason Mrs. Bowen chose to live in 1127? Was I drawn to the north side of house by the only feeling of welcome I had experienced in the home? Was there some small voice whispering inside my head that was directing me to choose the north side? Perhaps there was. Looking back through many years spent there, I can honestly say that likelihood seems perfectly natural.

Figure 2: The stairwell, 1973. The space that offered a
place for a restroom once the post and railing had been
removed and two walls with a door were installed.

Figure 3: The Stairwell from above showing bare wood
steps and the window of the door at the foot of the stairwell
in the first-floor hallway.

3

The Fixer-upper

Using an old-fashioned skeleton key, I unlocked the front door on the north side, 1125, and stepped inside for the first time. My attention was at first held by that door. It was a masterpiece of low security. The skeleton lock was the only lock on the door. In addition to that problem, the entire upper panel of the door was a large pane of glass. As I stood there looking at the first thing I came across within the fabric of the building and finding it to be totally inadequate for my purpose, a slightly uneasy feeling crept into me. "What have I done?" I asked myself. "Have I bought a renovation nightmare?" I closed the door and decided I had better get a more positive attitude established before I started kicking myself. I made a mental note to make the doors and windows a first priority for security purposes. Soon, the place would be filling up with some very expensive items. After taking a deep breath or two, I turned around and began my first tour of the place.

The room I was in was the living room, or parlor, as it was once known as. The dingy off-white walls produced a pall of eerie sadness. The same color was used on the walls of the hall just beyond the doorway straight across the room from where I stood. To my right was a double window that reduced the usefulness of the wall for my purposes but was of great value to the room when it was a parlor, adding natural light to augment the gaslight that once hung from the ceiling. This had been replaced by an electric light at some point in time, but the gas pipe was left in the ceiling to verify the presence of the gaslight. I decided the windows would have to be closed off, as would all windows on the first floor except for two that were set into the wall on the Twentieth Street side of the house. I needed security more than I needed natural light. Artificial lighting would be a major consideration in this place, where it had not been important before.

Diagonally across the room from the front door was a fireplace with a very plain surround that probably had ten or more coats of enamel paint on it. This last coat had yellowed to reduce the appeal of the poor thing even more than the shape alone afforded. The fireplace itself was designed to resemble a coal-burning grate. In its day, the gas stove was a modern marvel. One just had to turn the valve and light the hissing gas. For those who could afford the changeover from coal to gas, the improvement in convenience and warmth must have been heavenly. I stood there in the middle of the room looking at the fireplace, trying to imagine how it would have looked glowing in the darkness of a deep winter evening. To sit in a rocker there beside that "new age" fire, perhaps listening to a program on the radio, or a joke told by a friend on the couch nearby; that would have been a good way to end any day.

Then my wondering mind returned to the dingy room on a cold, damp, gray day, and the eerie gloom returned. The fireplace with its yellowed surround would have to be removed. In fact, the chimney that occupied the corner of the room would have to go as well. Space would have to be found in each room. A fireplace that cut off one whole corner would not be an asset that I could afford.

I looked at the dark oak trim around the room that formed the door facings and baseboards that would have been an attractive feature throughout the office, but all this woodwork would have to be refinished first, and I had no time for that. I reluctantly decided to commit the sin of painting all the woodwork in order to save time. I noted that the solid wood doors were fir or pine, not oak, and the floors were also pine. This was an obvious cost saving for the original builder and a slight problem for me. All rooms would have to have new flooring, which I decided would be laid over the pine.

I think Mrs. Bowen was perhaps the only owner/renter who lived in the building. For the other owners, the property was a business venture, and features such as pine flooring did not matter to them. By the time Mrs. Bowen took possession of the house, wall-to-wall carpets had come into vogue, and the pine flooring was conveniently covered by them, but only on her side, not the north side.

I passed through the front room and entered the hallway that led straight to the dining room. To my right was a door that led to the outside. This door was an exact duplicate of the front door, another security risk, and also a great loss of heat through the large single-pane window set into the top panel and a virtual breezeway resulting from the loose fit. I imagined how easy it would be for anyone to enter by that door with just a skeleton key, which was extremely common even as late as 1973. Since the door was located halfway from either end of the house, one could enter and leave without being seen night or day, with only a little luck needed. Later, I would learn that I was not the only one to come to that conclusion. At that point, I made a mental note to close off all first-floor windows and doors in the place except the front and back doors, and the two front windows. This way, security would be greatly increased. I had already decided to have rock wool blown into the walls to provide insulation, and the removal of all those windows and doors would improve the effect of the rock wool.

To my left was a small space created by the stairwell that wrapped around the walls as it ascended to the second-floor hallway directly above me. I imagined this area was where the telephone was kept. A small chair, a table, and a lamp would have been the only furniture needed. In its earliest years, the phone would have been on the wall, a wooden box with a speaking cone and earpiece made of vulcanite. Later, pillar phones would be the first to occupy the tiny table. This arrangement would have carried through the years with changes in furniture styles and phone designs. From these ruminations, I returned to the scene at hand—a dingy space at the bottom of a grim stairwell. Suddenly an idea came to me: the space would be perfect for the public restroom. I made another mental note. Close in the space and add plumbing.

Placing my hand on the cap of the newel post, I looked up into the stairwell. It seemed harsh to the extent of cruelty. The bare wood of the railings and steps seemed to hide a secret. For a moment, I thought I could hear whispering, faint and far away. That passed. I looked up into the vault of the staircase toward the ceiling with its porcelain light fixture and a single bulb that was shaded by a milk-glass canopy. The fixture seemed to be extremely far away. I assumed the stark angles of the steps and railings formed an illusion that pushed up the actual height of the ceiling to an apparent distance that was much higher. It was as if the walls stretched upward as one looked up.

The walls of the stairwell were painted an ugly shade of turquoise that had a coating of soot built up from years of neglect. They would have to be cleaned and repainted some other color. The ceiling was painted the same color as the walls, which I concluded, gave the impression of the increased height as one looked up into the space.

I stood there for several minutes with my hand on the newel post looking at the scene. But there was something going on that I could not figure out. The thought of whispering and soft shuffling came back to me. The total quiet of the house would amplify any sound I heard, or thought I heard. Something unseen dwelled up there in that angular space. In the tomb-like stillness, I thought I could hear breathing.

I snapped out of that unproductive state of mind and glanced beyond the open doorway into the dining room. I determined I would think about those odd impressions at a later date, when I had the time. Right then, I did not. As I stepped into the dining room, I turned and looked back into the hallway. Perhaps someday I would uncover a secret that was kept in that area, for whatever reason.

The remaining two rooms on the first floor were the dining room and the kitchen beyond that. Off from the kitchen was a small utility room that appeared to be an addition that had been built onto the house fairly recently. I decided the utility room would be removed. The construction was not well conceived, leaving it shaky and more of a hazard than an asset. As I made my way back through the kitchen and into the dining room, I noticed on the inner wall two gas lines. The fixtures had been removed long ago, but at one time, there had been two gas wall sconces and on the same wall in the dining room on the other side. That, and a gaslight hanging from the ceiling would have added an air of elegance to the room for the families who took their meals there years ago. A small door opened to a pantry with a very low ceiling, which was tucked under the landing of the stairwell. I looked inside. That would be a great place for kids to hide, I thought.

I went through the hallway and living room and went out onto the front porch. I made a quick mental list of the steps needed to bring that structure down. It would have to be carried away from the back of the house, so the entire thing would need to be hauled back there, piece by piece.

I made up a list of contractors to meet with and discuss the single-story room that would be added to the front once the porch was out of the way. I assumed that I could reduce my costs by doing the demolition myself. This would add a great deal of total area of floor space. I planned to set up this construction while my parents and I would work on the interior rooms converting them into office facilities.

31

The consultations with the contractors turned out to be a series of disappointments. All the estimates were far out of range of the budget that I had to work with. So my floor plan had to be reexamined. Somewhere, space had to be found that did not exist without the addition. The only answer at the time was to move more of the facility onto the second floor. All this would work, up until the time my practice grew enough to develop the need for a hygienist. Where would that operatory be located? For a short time, the hygienist's operatory and an auxiliary waiting room for her use would have to be set up on the second floor. These problems meant that I would likely be unable to rent out the other side of the building and would instead need it to expand my facilities.

Dad and I were not allowed to install any of the electrical or plumbing lines. Licensed professionals would have to do that. I decided it would be best to plumb all of the building on both sides and install wiring in both sides as well even though I still stubbornly clung to the idea I might rent out the south side at a later date. It turned out to be a wise decision. The electrical contractor we hired for the job set up the wiring diagram with a junction box on each side, with the south side left unconnected and without a meter. The north side would be run with separate lines and a meter. The head electrician on the crew doing the installation was a barrel-chested, rough-talking, crusty old geezer who had the gift of gab. With an ever-present lit cigarette jammed between two fingers on his left hand, he would tell endless tales about his childhood during the roaring twenties. He told me that he remembered my house from those turbulent times. He said he was a runner for a bootlegger in Huntington, Ashland, and Chesapeake. As he described his job, runners were boys who stood on the running boards of the cars that were used to make deliveries. The boys clung to the cars as they drove to their destinations. A worker in the back seat sorted the orders and handed them to the runners as they arrived at the addresses. The kid would run with the bottles, make the delivery, and return with the cash. Once on the runner board, off they would go. He said tips were usually very good. He told me that he had stopped at my house on many occasions, and as he put it, "They had some wild parties back then. People would roll up the carpet, move out the furniture, except for the Victrola, and dance the night away. The flappers wore short dresses and short haircuts." That was the first time I had anyone tell me anything about the early years of the house. Standing there listening to the old fellow tell us of his experiences in the place, I could easily see in my mind how it might have looked and sounded.

Dad and I began on the windows and doors that were a security risk. We cut a sheet of plywood and nailed it to the front door on the south side, but the windows were removed, boxed in, and closed up with plywood in anticipation of the insulation that would soon be blown into the walls. Once that was done, we addressed the interior of the house. At that point, the furnace and ductwork were not installed, so we had power, but no heat. As the days moved along, it got colder in the place, and we set up a camp heater to work with, but it could only heat one room.

I set about cleaning and painting the stairwell. I decided to use beige to cover the ill-chosen turquoise color scheme. The beige brought a warmth into the space and lightened up what had been so sad and dingy. As I was painting the three walls of the stairwell, I noticed that there were no carpet nail holes on any of the steps, or on the landing. The stairwell had never been carpeted. The dark-brown wood that formed the railings and steps had always been just as I saw them, angular, hard, unyielding. A fall down those stairs would hurt. As I thought of that fact, a strange feeling crept back—the one I had on that first day when I stood at the foot of the stairs looking up into the well. Then I began to get that strange feeling one gets when he knows he is being watched. Another feeling crept into my awareness—one of dread. That feeling awakened the memory of the first time I saw the house. I began searching my recollections, and soon I was filling in details of that night, as I splashed beige paint on the walls without stopping for lunch. The memories fed the feelings I was having as I painted. I remembered something about the house as I looked at it on that night; something was telling me to stay away. I remembered vividly that feeling, and here it was again. Something was rejecting me in a very real way, and yet something else had invited me here in a warm and friendly way. Slowly, I pieced together the two sensations. The welcome and the rejection were from different sources. What could that mean? It was apparent that something of a dynamic was going on there. Something was looking at me. Something that I could not see. And there was something else. Something was hiding, and from it came the sensation of both pain and sadness, and yet, that source was also the one of welcome. Two sources of some sort of mystical power were at work. One was clearly a threat, and the other was pleading and in need of help of some kind. It was like a faint cry one hears without being able to make out the words.

With so many problems I was dealing with, I found it very strange that such mental meanderings would not only come to mind but that for a short time, would actually crowd out the confusion and pressing problems I was sorting out during that period in my life.

4

By the Pricking of My Thumbs

I was buying equipment, paint, flooring, fixtures, and furnishings for rooms that had not yet been stripped down to the bare surfaces so that they could be put back together in their new configurations. As I tore away the existing interiors and hauled away what had greeted me on my first tour of the place, I was in endless conversation with everyone involved in the project about paint schemes for the walls, which should have paper and which should be plastered, where the counters would go, where the commode would be located, where the x-ray panels would be placed, where ducts would pass through walls along with wiring conduit and plumbing lines. Each room presented its own set of challenges of space and traffic flow. I was up at seven o'clock each morning and worked straight through until three o'clock the following morning. There was no time for anything other than the evolution of the house into an office. Without the help of my parents, it would not have been possible.

Dad and I set up a table saw in the former dining room. Around that central piece of equipment were stacked construction materials of every kind. In almost every room were stacks of similar materials awaiting their turn to become part of the fabric of the office. Plumbers, foundation repairmen, electricians, and city code examiners all crowded into the limited spaces left unoccupied. We soon discovered that there were indeed problems we did not anticipate finding their way into the process. The costs were soaring in spite of our best efforts to cut corners wherever we could. Walls thought to be sound were found to have water damage, and the whole foundation had to be supported with concrete piers to prevent the center of the building from sinking. The city officials did their best to prevent the project from starting in the first place. They presented a list of demands that would have been funny had they not been so adamant about them. Finally, after many weeks of wrangling with them, we had our permits from on-high to go ahead with the work. Our most difficult problem was in the cost of the materials. There was a plywood shortage, a copper shortage, and porcelain products shortage, stud shortage, gypsum shortage. As a result of these reductions in availability for nearly everything we needed to buy, our budget was thrown to the wind. The only bargain we found was our own cheap labor, and an iron will to get around all the obstacles that were set in front of us. The two fireplaces in the front rooms were taken out and the chimney common to both of them was removed. This was done by my father and me. I went up on the roof and began throwing bricks down the chimney as I pried them loose. I only dropped three at a time so that Dad would not have to worry about

37

having a brick hit his hands. He pulled away the dropped bricks, and then I would join him in the front room to carry out each pile that had accumulated. Pile after pile was taken out to the front yard until the entire chimney was outside the house. A man who wanted some clean fill material for a construction site he was working on hauled the entire stack of bricks away. The fireplace surrounds were likewise taken away by a handyman who knew of an apartment building owner who wanted them. And so it went. All the large items we took out had someone ready to take them away. Even the plaster and lathe we took from the walls were of some use to someone. A farmer took one of the two claw-foot bathtubs to use as a watering trough for his cows. It scooted like a bobsled down the stairs and out the front door onto the bed of his waiting truck.

One evening, Dad and I were in the dining room measuring a sheet of plywood which was going to replace an oddly shaped area of flooring in the front room. We were quietly measuring and scribing the lines for the piece, not saying much to each other at the time. We wanted to get it right the first time since we were getting tired. Suddenly we heard the sounds of someone with heavy shoes stomping around, throwing objects against the walls, and kicking things around in the dining room just opposite to us on the south side of the house.

We both froze and looked at each other with surprise on both our faces. Dad picked up a hammer, and I grabbed a crowbar. Someone was on the other side of the duplex, but how? We went out onto the front porch, and as we crossed it to the front door on the south side, we listened for the sounds of our intruder. We had to pry loose the boards that we had nailed across the front door. I was looking through the large window in the door as we loosened the last board. I could not see anyone inside or any sign that he had a flashlight.

Dad had brought a flashlight, and he turned it on as we stepped inside the living room. It was dark and cold. There was suddenly an eerie silence to the place. The flashlight caused stark shadows to dart everywhere as Dad trained the light about the room. The irregular shapes of the construction materials set in high piles created the shadows. We went into the hallway with Dad's flashlight darting about, casting the only light we had quickly from place to place.

Nothing was out of place. Nothing was harmed. We had expected to see cans of paint broken open, boxes of nails spilled, and stacks of studs all askew. Nothing was out of place. "I don't get it," I said. It didn't make sense. We both heard things that were heavy hitting the wall and then the floor.

"How did he do that?" Dad asked, mostly to himself. We searched the entire place, room by room. There was no sign of anything that could account for what we both had heard. When we returned to the dining room, I examined the wall that was struck so many times with a heavy object of some kind, and yet the plaster was not damaged. We were astounded. There was no answer. "Well, whoever it was, he went up the stairs to the bathroom up there. He got up on the bathtub and lifted himself up into the ceiling hatch. He could hide there and leave after we leave," he said, still mostly to himself.

"But how did he make all that noise? Why would he do that? How did he get in?" I asked. Dad admitted that whoever it was was a real practical joker.

"He has to get here before we do and leave after we do. He hides out in the attic," Dad asserted with enough authority to convince himself. After thinking about it for a minute, I decided there must be a better explanation. But what? How did he make all that noise without disturbing anything? Nothing added up.

On the way home, Dad came up with a theory to explain the noise. The joker had used a single stud. Swinging it in all directions, he would hit the wall with glancing blows that would do very little damage to the plaster. Swinging it like a baseball bat he could hit the floor and other stacks of supplies without disturbing them. He could then lay the stud back in the stack where we had placed them, and scamper up the stairs, into the bathroom, up on the tub, through the ceiling hatch while we were prying boards off the door. He would have time to do that. "Do you know anyone who would do that?" I asked. Dad concluded someone wanted us to walk away from the project for some reason.

While he may have been right, there was another possibility. I chose not to bring it up right then. Dad was an extremely pragmatic man who loved the physical sciences. Math and physics were his joy. He was a self-taught student. He loved astronomy. He read about all aspects of astronomy in textbooks and periodicals. His acumen on the subject was impressive. Science is the only way to look for answers to questions about almost any subject. That was Dad's mantra. He had made a reflecting telescope from scratch. He even ground his own lenses and mirrors. For an oak tripod to support the telescope, he cut up a kitchen table. With this telescope made by his own hands, we could see the surface of Jupiter with its giant red spot and multiple bands of russet color. He was definitely a man of science. His purely scientific mind would not countenance any concept that was not clearly understandable through calculation and experimentation.

As time went on, I began to have accidents. One expects accidents when using tools while getting very little sleep, but some of my mishaps started me thinking about the place. I added up the loud noises Dad and I had heard with several odd accidents I was having and the weird sensations I had felt while painting the stairwell. While some of my injuries were the direct result of sleep deprivation, others were not. Two examples can be used to illustrate the incidents that were occurring constantly but forming into two distinct categories.

An easily explainable incident occurred when I was removing the front porch. I had taken away the banisters, and flooring was taken up along with the joists that supported the floor. These were lying on the ground right where I had dropped them. They were scattered there in a general disarray. The roof was supported by a series of two-by-fours. I removed the roofing shingles and sheeting boards beneath them. They were scattered around the outer perimeter of the porch foundations. I was standing on the rafters and taking them out one-by-one and throwing them out with the shingles. It was raining and dark. I slipped and fell from the rafters to the boards on the ground below me. I remember the wind rushing past my ears as I hurled

41

toward the boards and nails. I threw away the crowbar as I slipped.

I fell back first, landing on my shoulder. I felt the nails go into me immediately. They pierced my calves, thighs, hips, back, and scalp. I waited a few seconds before trying to get up. I needed to check for broken bones first. Finding none, I rolled to my right as the nails came out of all areas except for two or three in my back. I stood up and pulled those boards loose. Those nails were all the way into my shoulder blades.

I went into the house and found a medicine chest that would someday be placed in one of the bathrooms. Setting it up on the table saw, I made a quick check of my back. To my surprise, none of the nail holes were bleeding much. I determined no large vessels had been hit, so I put my clothes back on and decided to finish the job, for the following day would find me with some very sore muscles. The job was finished, and by the dawn light, all boards and shingles were in piles in back of the building ready for removal. All that remained of the porch were the outline of the foundation blocks, and the concrete steps. These would soon exit the premises by way of a sledgehammer and a friend with a truck. All this could have happened to anyone doing a similar job. No mystery.

The following is an example of the sort of thing experienced but without a plausible explanation. The flooring in the back two rooms on the first floor required considerable attention before the tiles could be put down. I was on my knees one morning, getting the floors ready for their new surfacing of vinyl tiles. There were stacks of boards in three corners of the back room and two in the middle room. Out of the corner of my eye, as I worked in a crouching position on one knee, I saw a stack of boards suddenly hurl from their resting place and pummel my back. I jumped to my feet to find two of them stuck to me. More nails! This odd occurrence repeated on two more occasions. By that time, I was alert to the sudden movement of any boards.

Later that day, I decided to remove the boards from the building and stack them in our makeshift lumberyard in the back of the building. My parents joined me that evening as I was finally putting the finishing touches on the floors of those two back rooms. My mother came into the room where I was kneeling over a plywood joint that needed some spackle applied. She was carrying a fresh batch of boards into the room to stack them in a corner. Before I was aware that she was coming into the room, I saw out of my peripheral vision the moving boards as they alone were entering the room. I jumped to my feet to get out of the way. It was an instant reaction that startled my mother.

She froze, looking at me with a face full of questions. "What are you doing?" she asked. I explained about the boards "falling" out of the corners all day, and how the nails in them had managed to scratch me several times. "Bill, do you think this place is haunted?" I nodded in agreement. We recounted on our fingers the very strange things that had occurred while we were working on the place. These occurrences were beyond explainable in any way except that unseen forces were at work, and the changes we were making were not wanted. We discussed how tired we all were from the exhausting pace we had been keeping, and how even that could not explain away the strange things that were going on. I told her about the odd feelings I had noticed while in the stairwell. She said she had not noticed anything like that anywhere in the place, but I knew that she understood what I was relating to her, and she believed me. We tried to open the subject to Dad, but he was not receptive. He concluded we were tired and had let overactive imaginations take over when all was easily explained; however, he never came up with those "easy explanations."

Figure 4: The newly opened office, viewed from my apartment over a grocery store across Twentieth Street, 1974.

5

The Little Girl

I found a dental office of sorts that I was using to keep my practice together as much as possible while I struggled to get my office open. The office I was using had belonged to another dentist who had died. His equipment was at least fifty years old, with all the odd quirks old equipment has when it is running on makeshift repairs and patches. I discovered the first thing I would have to do was to learn the rules of engagement with my very temperamental dental equipment. Leaks and blown fuses were the normal operational status with this grizzled old codger of a dental unit. As I was shutting down the office for the day, I heard the unmistakable sound of splashing water. This was not a little drip. This was a real leak! I raced about looking for the valve to turn the waterline to the unit off. I could not find it. The floor was starting to look like a small pond.

Then I remembered that the office space below me was occupied by a lawyer. Down to his office I ran. I burst into his private office where I found him practicing on a violin. He seemed to be in his own little world of classical music. "Quick, where is the turn-off for the water in the office above?" I said as fast as I was running. "Oh no! Not again!" he exclaimed as he threw aside his violin and bow and sprang to his feet. He ran into what looked like a utility room. On the back wall was a confusing tangle of valves and pipes. He could not remember which one it was. I jumped in front of him and began to turn all of them off as quickly as I could. "Good idea!" he said. We finally shut down the entire building of offices and apartments. I turned to his private office. The sound of dripping water had spurred my attention toward that area.

Sure enough, water was dripping onto his desk which was completely covered with all sorts of papers and books. "Oh no!" cried the lawyer. We both raced for his desk and began throwing everything to the floor. He placed his waste container right in the center of his desk for what was now a small stream of water. As we picked up the papers from the floor and separated the dry ones from the wet ones, we began to chat. "Got a clothesline?" I asked. I learned that leaks from the dental office above had occurred all too often when the office was occupied, so when the dentist passed away, the lawyer assumed that problem was solved. I was an unexpected setback. We talked a while and became acquainted with our respective life stories, and then I left his office to return to the mess upstairs, which required a lot of mopping, and then to the task of renovation at my own dental office. Because of the time lost with the leak, I would be starting my work much later than I had planned.

My schedule was altered by my office hours. I worked on my patients from eight o'clock in the morning to twelve noon. Then I would rush to the construction site and work there until two or three o'clock in the morning. After a brief nap, my next day would begin. Dad worked at a factory on the evening shift. At that time, he was foreman in the machine shop. He had worked as a machinist for many years there, and that was where his heart was, but he was nearing the end of his career and the position of foreman would bring better pay and benefits. He arrived at my dental office at about one o'clock in the morning and worked with my mother and me until we could go no further. That was usually at two or three o'clock, but as we got closer to our opening day, we were working around the clock. The day I first worked in my office on my patients was April 15, 1974. I remember inserting my key into the lock on that first day. The feeling was unforgettable; after two decades of use, the door was replaced, but I still have that lock and that key. I completely forgot about that day being tax day until about three in the afternoon. A patient casually mentioned something about paying his taxes. Panic set in. But that is another story.

At last, the office was complete enough to open it for practice. Work on the building would continue for many years to come, but at last, I was treating patients in my own office using my own equipment. I had a waiting room with a small business office partitioned off; a single operatory and restroom completed the first floor. The back room was converted into the workplace for after-hours work that continued on the second-floor remodeling process. The exterior of the building was now covered by aluminum siding that neatly hid the blocked-in windows and doors.

The time had come to do something with the stairwell. The steps, which had never been carpeted, were now covered with the same carpeting that covered the waiting room and hallway. The bland beige walls needed help. I decided to paper the walls with newspaper clippings. This would take a long time to complete, but for some reason, this was a project I felt I had to do. I obtained stacks of newspapers from Nick's News, a newsstand located downtown, and began searching through them for interesting articles to paste on the walls—hundreds of them. I used wheat paste to affix the newsprint pieces to the walls. To be able to reach the higher areas of the walls, I put together a makeshift scaffold that went around the three walls starting at the top step. From the landing, this scaffold was a bit over six feet high. As it went around to the banister rail, it went up to about ten feet above the landing, but at that point, it was over the first flight of steps from the first floor. It was not safe, but the ten-inch-wide planks were all I had to make it with. At that point, I had become used to taking risks in the interest of getting the office complete as soon as possible.

I was working on the scaffold. It was after eleven o'clock. The only sounds in the office were my movements on the scaffold, the rustle of the papers, and the soft "slushing" sounds of the paste being applied to the clippings and the walls. This process produced a soothing atmosphere that actually provided a break for me similar to the way one feels at the beach with the sounds of the wind and the waves. As I stood on the part of the scaffold that stretched across the far wall, I became aware of a subtle change in the light, or rather the air around me. There was a steady increase of static electricity. The level of light seemed to decrease, but the change was not caused by the ceiling light dimming, for that light was above and behind

49

me, high against the ceiling. It was rather a shift in the ambient light, a strange murky gray veil enveloping me. It was as if a three-dimensional shadow had filled the entire space of the stairwell, a darkening of the air itself. It was as if the air had become thick. The static charge increased even more. I stopped working and stood still on the board, wondering if something was wrong with me. I began mentally checking my physical systems, thinking I was about to have a medical emergency, but except for that feeling of static electrical charge, I was fine. But the hair on my scalp was standing up.

Then I felt a presence in the area. It was behind me. The ten-inch board made turning around very difficult because it was so narrow and too close to the wall for my shoulder width. Finally I managed to twist around and turn my back to the wall, and I looked up. That was when I saw her.

She was standing at the top of the stairs just outside the doorway to the front bedroom. Quietly looking at me with big brown eyes, she was standing in a gray mist. Then she vanished. Just as I was able to see her and recognize what I was seeing, she was gone. My blood turned to ice water. My knees buckled and down from the plank I came, half falling, half jumping. No sooner than I had crashed onto the landing I found myself taking giant leaps down the lower flight of steps, through the dark hallway, across the waiting room, and out through the front door.

Outside, there were people in cars on Twentieth Street calmly waiting for the traffic light to change. I stepped away from the office and looked at the front facade. My heart rate was starting to slow down. Nothing about the outside of the building betrayed what I had just experienced. I felt my pulse now that my heart was no longer pounding in my throat. The rate was over one hundred. Strength was returning, but I was not ready to go back inside to turn off the lights. I pulled my keys from my pocket and locked the door. I stood there for several minutes sorting through my thoughts. I noticed that I was very cold, in spite of the very warm night air. Some symptoms of the shock still lingered, but I felt I could walk across Twentieth Street, the bandy-legged feeling was gone.

At that time, I was renting an apartment that was above a grocery store located directly across the street, Holland's Grocery. I made it to the side entrance and climbed the stairs to my apartment. From the front room I could look directly across the street through a large picture window. I stood at that window for a long time looking at my office across the way. I began piecing together the experience. I went through each step analyzing what was seen and felt. Then I concentrated on the girl, trying to remember each detail about her, and that strange vapor that surrounded her. She was very thin, sickly, with dark hair that fell about her shoulders in a matted tangle dampened by sweat. Her thin face was dominated by huge dark-brown eyes that yearned for something. Understanding? Sympathy? Her eyes had dark circles around them, the eyes of desperate illness and pain. Her thin lips never moved to speak, but she seemed to be on the verge of crying. What could she harbor in that frail body? Some secret was there. A secret she desperately needed to expose. Her frail neck seemed too small for her head. Her delicate, feeble arms and shoulders formed a frame that could easily be broken in a bear hug. She wore a white slip or nightgown with tiny shoulder straps. The wreath-like mist that surrounded her had made a fog-like barrier that shrouded her legs, so I do not know if the slip was full length or short. The dark aura that filled the whole stairwell around me seemed, in reflection, to be part of her. I think her energy had made that dark air, the gray-white mist around her, and the brief image I saw. It may have taken a great deal from her to produce all that effect. For that reason, perhaps, I did not see her again for several days.

One thing was for certain. The office really was haunted! I had seen the ghost of a girl with dark hair. In the ensuing weeks, as I completed the papering of the walls of the stairwell, I witnessed the girl many times. The aura that I experienced the first time was greatly reduced, as was the gray fog that swirled around her. During those later "revealings," she would simply stand there for an instant and be gone. Never moving, never making a sound, she just stood there looking at me. It was still unnerving, but not frightening as with the first time I saw her. As I saw her repeatedly, I was able to assemble a memory-based image in my head that was more detailed; from the overlapping visual images, I produced one highly resolved imprint of her in my mind. But that was all I had of her, and I did not know why she appeared to me. It did not occur to me to try to talk to her. I assumed that when she vanished, she was gone both from sight and sound, so talking to her would not make sense since she had apparently left the area. Later on, the little girl stopped appearing. I assumed she was no longer there in the stairwell, at first, but later, I came to think she might still be there, or somewhere near there.

I began to wonder if she just wanted to be sure I knew she was in the stairwell. Perhaps that was all there was to it. And yet, that could not be what she wanted, for she seemed to be suffering.

Was my failure to understand her causing her to have more suffering? I did not have enough to go on.

6

Something Wicked This Way Comes?

Later, I heard sounds. These sounds were clearly not made by a little girl. They were loud sounds. Sounds like the ones Dad and I had heard that one night that we could not figure out. Now they were back. But now the sounds were taking on a pattern. This repetition of loud sounds was heard once every month or so. The sounds always began on the second floor in the back rooms. The slam of a door. Then the sounds of heavy footfalls intermixed with more slammed doors. The footfalls often descended the stairs. On the landing, sometimes there would be the sounds of stomping boots. A few times, the loud footfalls descended the lower flight of stairs. Then all would be quiet. An eerie quiet after such loud noises.

One night, as the owner of the alarm company that was connected to the office worked at the alarm center on an amplifier, he heard on the speaker relaying sounds from my office the sounds of slamming doors and stomping feet. He froze his position and looked in the direction of the woman who monitored the speaker boxes. She saw his questioning expression and answered him, saying, "That's the ghost in the dentist's office." She calmly reported this information with a matter-of-fact way that brought even more expressions from the face of the owner.

"Ghost! What are you talking about?" he asked with a tightening in his throat.

"That sound of the slamming doors and the heavy footsteps," she answered. "Those are the sounds of a ghost in the office. We listen for any more sounds, but there never are any more. They just start and end like that."

The owner told me he was speechless. A chill went up his spine. He said the microphone on the second floor in the hallway had picked up the unmistakable sounds of doors slamming very hard, and the distinct sounds of heavy shoes walking in a sloppy stumbling fashion toward, under, and then past the microphone. He told me that he had never experienced anything like that in all his years in the alarm business. These sounds were picked up with the type of system used by the company at that time. This system was installed in 1976. It involved a series of microphones placed in various areas of the office. The office was literally wired for sound.

Each evening before leaving, I turned the alarm system on. I would announce who I was and give out a number that verified that I was who I said I was. Hearing this, the person who was monitoring the system checked my personal identification number and pressed a button at her desk. This caused a green light to flash on my alarm panel, and I knew that I was cleared to exit the office. When I entered the office, I repeated the name and identification number, and upon seeing the green light flash, I would turn the alarm off. While the alarm was armed, the person in the room with the speakers could hear anything that occurred in all the businesses and homes she had speakers for in the room. When a sound was picked up, a light came on at the speaker box that was activated. She could increase the volume if she wished. I was often awakened at night, usually at two or three o'clock in the morning with a call from the alarm company to come to the office to check the place out with some police officers. Back then, they would let me accompany them as they flashed their flashlights around in the dark rooms. We never saw anything. Just a dark dental office that had some rooms in the midst of remodel. The police and I would have conversations about what caused the alarms. With unsettling calm, I would tell them that the place is haunted, and they were hearing my ghost. That usually ended our conversation.

After this had gone on for about two years, the police department had had enough. They contacted the alarm company and told them that they would have to come up with some way to end the false alarms at my office. They backed up their statement with the warning that if they did not comply, citations would be given for the false alarms. That prompted the alarm company to adopt a "ghost policy." When something was heard going on in my office, they would turn up the volume and listen carefully. If nothing else was heard, they would call neither the police nor me. From that time onward, I was able to sleep through the night without being called out to the office.

By this time, there was growing common knowledge that there were ghosts in the office. I was certain that the stories that were told years before about the place had to be true, but I wondered if what I had experienced were the things that prompted the stories told so long before. Did Mrs. Bowen know about the sights and sounds? Did her renters? Or was her demeanor rigorous enough to cause the spirits to hide away, waiting for a more receptive person to wander into the place? Was this the reason she chose to live in the side of the duplex that seemed to have less activity? Possibly. I will never know.

Who was the dull brute? Why did he break the silence of the night by stomping around and slamming doors? Those who heard the sounds all wondered just what did it all mean? I had no idea. Looking back on that time, I often wonder how I could have been so stupid. I named the ghost that made the noises Big Guy. One thing I was able to figure out. Big Guy seemed to have frightened away the little girl. I never saw her again.

Figure 5: Portrait of Lavina Wall within a mist encircling her as she stood at the doorway to her room at the top of the stairwell.

7

A Whisper from the Past, Lavina

For several years, all these strange happenings slowed down but never stopped entirely. My daughter, Carey, saw the little girl as she sat in the waiting room looking through the doorway into the hallway and the foot of the stairwell. The little girl appeared to Carey in the hallway. She was holding on to the framing of the doorway and swinging back and forth as she looked at Carey. Her head was tilted back so that her long dark-brown hair was swinging wildly. Then she seemed to fly up the stairs, out of sight in a flash. She appeared from time to time to several children on or near the stairwell.

A short time ago, a woman told me she had been a patient when I was involved in a program for kindergarten school children. The year was about 1975. She passed the stairwell on her way to operatory 1 and glanced up the stairs and saw a little girl wearing a slip standing on the landing. Later, she told her mother about the sighting, to which her mother said that it was just her imagination. Her mother had passed by the stairwell with her daughter's hand in hers, and *she* saw no one on the landing. In spite of her mother's refusal to accept the story, she held to the belief that the little girl on the landing in a slip was really there, not imagined.

In the late 1970s, a patient, Mrs. Andre, told me a startling story. She said she had been in the office once many years before when it was a duplex residence. She was there to pay a visit to a relative by marriage. The family consisted of a mother and two daughters. One of the daughters, the younger one, was seriously ill. She died a few days after the visit. This story piqued my interest immediately. I asked her when that happened. After thinking for a few minutes, she said that it was about 1925 as near as she could remember. She said the family told her that they thought she had died from a case of appendicitis. She said when she looked into the bedroom where the girl lay, it was such a pitiful sight. She was in terrible pain. Her hair was all twisted and matted with perspiration. Mrs. Andre said she realized she should not try to talk to the girl, so she just turned and came back down the stairs to the living room. I asked her to describe the girl. "Oh, she was a sad, pitiful little thing. She was suffering so much. It was just awful."

There it was. There was the reason the girl had appeared to me. She wanted someone to realize she had died up there in the front bedroom after suffering greatly. Perhaps she had drifted into a coma and did not realize she had died. Perhaps she was trying to find out what I was doing in her house, in her stairwell. At last I had a possible clue as to who this ghost was and why she showed herself to me. Mrs. Andre described the girl just the way I had seen her. Her matted hair, dark circles around large brown eyes, thin cheeks, and a tiny, thin mouth. We were both affected by her appallingly sad expression. I was running all these thoughts through my mind when, suddenly, they jerked to a stop. There must be more information! The golden piece of information was the name. She said the little girl's name was Lavina Wall. With that, I was certain I knew who my little ghost was. I knew something about the time in which she lived and about when she died.

Then Mrs. Andre told me a story about Lavina's family and how she came to live in my building back in the late 1920s. She told me the story, as well as she was able to remember, as it was told to her by her husband, who in turn learned of it from Lavina's family members. Later there would be investigations over several years that would establish areas of inaccuracy, but Mrs. Andre was relating a story from many years in her own past, and it was not all from firsthand, so I think she should be allowed latitude in veracity. One thing I am certain of—her version of the story of Lavina's death was based on the truth as she remembered it. Only later would I learn that the most crucial information about Lavina's death was withheld from her, and perhaps, her husband as well. So what Mrs. Andre was told was part truth and part lies. The lies were developed as a cover story to protect the family from shame and the sister and mother from further harm. As a result of the alteration of what actually happened, the soul of a girl was trapped on a stairwell for decades, and the soul of a hulk of a man was there to torment her and others. The story as it was given to me went as follows:

In Lawrence County, Ohio, the family of Lavina Wall lived on a farm. The abusive drunkard of a father seemed to harbor a hatred toward women. He was reported to say, "The only good woman you will ever find in the whole world would be a woman with hair on her palms." This strange demoralization of womanhood in general is one of the few lasting testimonials that he left to posterity, but it exposes his twisted mind better than any volumes of verbiage he could have left. His name was Cyrus Kemp Wall. He preferred to be called Kemp. That is why I will refer to him as Cyrus in this writing. Lavina's mother, Bernice, was constantly abused by Cyrus, and this abuse escalated when Cyrus became drunk, which was, apparently, often. There were two sons who probably were not direct targets of the father's wrath, but they moved away as soon as they were able. Bernice and her two daughters were planning their escape. They were hoarding meager stashes of money as they secretly made their plans. Then tragedy struck. Their farmhouse burned to the ground. In the fire, a child, a boy, perished. With what little they had, the three slipped away and wound up in the duplex at 1125 Twentieth Street.

Mrs. Andre continued with her story, telling me a bit about how Bernice and the older sister (she couldn't remember her name) worked as waitresses in a restaurant or diner in Huntington. Lavina worked at home, taking in jobs as a seamstress, but she was greatly affected by the death of her infant brother in the fire. She grieved for him and never came out of this melancholy. Then she became ill and died in the house in the front bedroom. The fire had precipitated their escape even though they were not quite ready at that point. That was the story as she remembered it. At the time she related the story to me she said that the years had dimmed her recall, and so some details might be blended with other memories, but she felt she was fairly accurate with it. The dates were where she was not at all certain of accuracy. She said she thought that the last time she saw Lavina, it had been very cold. For that reason, she thought it might have been during the winter months, perhaps February or early March.

After hearing her revelations, I felt I had all the information I needed. There was no reason to research the past. I knew what I had to know, and that was that. How wrong I was. I wondered why Lavina could not or would not speak. I decided that ghosts do not speak unless they have a great deal of strength, and this girl could not possess great strength. Only her face spoke to me, the dark, sad eyes pleading for understanding.

I decided there was one way to express to her that I did see her, and that I understood that she had suffered. I decided to paint her portrait. I would hang it in the stairwell, and if she ever returned, she would see it there and know that I could see her. Perhaps that would open some sort of dialogue between us in some form of sign language. Since words seemed to be eliminated as a means of communication for whatever reason, I ventured into nonverbal forms. I finished her portrait and mounted in an antique frame. I decided to hang the painting high on the wall in the stairwell. That would put it out of reach of anyone without a long ladder. It was not obvious in its high position.

At that time, the stairwell was often used by patients because I had located an operatory on the second floor with an adjacent waiting room for the hygienist. Her patients used the stairwell all day long. By placing the painting in that corner of the stairwell near the ceiling, the location was so unobtrusive no one noticed it, but I was certain Lavina could see it if she ever returned. The front bedroom where Lavina had died was now my private office. I did not hang the picture in there because I was at that time certain that she avoided that room. I thought it would be a place where she would remember only suffering and death. These were purely suppositions on my part.

8

The Heavy Steps on the Stairs: Big Guy

While my practice was steadily growing to the point of needing my hygienist on the first floor, my only solution was expansion into the other side of the duplex, because I wanted the hygiene operatory on the first floor and the current floor plan was inconvenient for everyone. No one liked the hygienist operatory on the second floor. By the close of the decade, all the operations having to do with our patients were performed on the first floor. The temporary rooms used by the hygienist were changed into sitting rooms. At times our patients would use these rooms as auxiliary waiting rooms when they wanted to be away from the waiting area on the first floor, so there was, and continues to be, some light traffic up and down the stairwell by our patients.

Even though I was sure the portrait would reconnect me with Lavina, I never saw her again. The one we called Big Guy, was, however, a presence that we could count on from time to time. My long hours had started up again with work on the rooms in the south side of the duplex. One-by-one, the rooms took on a finished appearance. Often, late at night, my work would be interrupted with the sounds of Big Guy as he banged and stomped around in the place. By that time, I was always relieved when I assured myself that the noises were not caused by some living person up to no good. But I had to stop working and check the office each time I heard him.

In 1981, February presented a perfect time for youngsters to test their skill and courage on sleds. One deep snow followed the other, an endless winter drudge. As snow piled up, so did the list of accidents. We saw adults with injuries sustained in falls and children who failed to stop their sleds in time. One mother brought me to the office late one evening with a son who had guided his sled right into a tree. We were all together in operatory 1. I had raised the chair to tabletop height and dropped it into a flat position much like an examination table. The boy was lying on the chair as I stood to his right. His mother was standing to his left near his head, holding his left hand. As I cleared away his injured tissues, sutured his inner lip, and repaired his broken teeth, we were not talking at all. The only sound was what I was making as I worked on the boy's mouth.

Then we all jumped to the sound of a big man stomping and banging on the walls as if he were carrying a heavy object as he descended the steps. His uncertain footfalls made sounds of a man very drunk. It was possible to hear his heavy boots impacting the carpeted treads, and the brushing of his arm and shoulder against the wall as if he was using it to keep himself from falling. The boy jerked a surprised glance at me with frightened eyes flashing. I looked at the mother who was pointing to the closed door with the hand with the bloody towel she had held to her son's mouth. She silently formed the words, "There's someone there!"

I was convinced that this time it might not be just Big Guy. It might be a thief who was headed our way. There was a scalpel on the instrument tray just behind the boy's head. As I grabbed it, the boy began scooting back from the chair and up onto the tray scattering instruments in both directions as he was now entirely on the counter behind the dental chair. His mother was in the process of joining him as I went around the chair to the closed door at the foot of the steps.

I gripped the scalpel and snatched the door open. I slashed the blade of the scalpel in an arc, determined to draw first blood in what would be a desperate clash. *Swish, swish*, I went in swashbuckling fashion, but there was no hulking adversary to be sliced. The hallway was empty. I ran through it into the waiting room and then through the business office. I checked to make sure the doors were locked. To my great relief, I realized it had been Big Guy and not some brute of an intruder. My relief was exhilarating. The prospect of not having to engage in a losing battle with someone twice my size made me almost giddy.

I returned to operatory 1 to the mother and son holding each other in a grip of fear. "It's okay. It was just my ghost," I said without thinking of how that sounded.

"Ghost!" they replied with faces that went from fear to horror. Down from the counter they came, grabbing coats and purse as they flashed past me, and out through the waiting room, office, and front door. I followed them out to their car as it sped away from the curb and trailed off into the dark, cold night. As I watched the red taillights ascend the hill on Norway Avenue, I thought that I did not handle that well. The traffic light in the intersection had changed from red to green, casting a festive glow on the snow that was piled up everywhere.

Once back inside, I looked around and shouted, "Thanks, Big Guy! Thanks a lot!" I figured I had just lost two patients. As it turned out, I only lost one. The son refused to enter the office ever again. The mother eventually did return. In fact, she went to work for me years later as an assistant. Rita would become acquainted with the hauntings again.

Figure 6: The lunch room. Paco's bedroom at an earlier time?
He skipped toward the saloon doors, turned left, and skipped
right through the refrigerator.

9

The Lighter Steps Upstairs, Paco

As work continued year after year, I was able to set schedules for myself so that I could work at a much slower pace than before. The panic to get rooms completed so that the office could be a place in which to practice dentistry had been left far behind. Now the work took on the air of hobby and not necessity. To this day, the place occupies my weekends often, but I can quit at any time I choose, without working harder the next night.

I decided to remove the center wall that separated the two middle rooms on the second floor. This would open up a large space and make it far easier to transfer from one side to the other. This would be a room that would be the full width of the office north to south. On the chosen Friday, after closing up the office, I began breaking the plaster from the lathe and pulling the lathe slats from the studs. A rather large pile of plaster bits was rising against the closed door that led to the back room. Since this process causes a lot of dust, I had placed a sheet across the doorway leading up the hallway to the front of the building. There was no way to go out of the room except through the hallway. The door to the front bedroom had been closed just in case dust made it past the sheet over the doorway that had no door to close it off. As progress went at a surprisingly fast pace, I had that part of the task completed. I decided to take a break. In the front room on that side, there was a long table, chairs, and a couch. We held staff meetings in there. I decided to lie down on the couch and relax a bit. I fell into a deep sleep in only a few seconds.

At about midnight, I was awakened by the sounds of rustling papers on the small desk against the wall across from the couch. The long table in the middle of the room blocked my view as I opened one eye and surveyed the semi-dark room. The streetlight outside cast dim light through the curtained windows. I could not see what was causing the noise, so I assumed that there must be a mouse searching for something to eat. "Sorry, little fellow, this place is void of snacks," I said softly. I decided I would set some live traps in the morning. I preferred to capture the mice in humane traps, take them away from the office, and let them go in a nearby thicket with a brook running through it.

Then I heard the unmistakable sound of footfalls on the creaky wooden boards of the floor in the room. That was no mouse. As quietly as possible, I stood up and listened, trying to locate where a larger pest might be located. After moments of listening intently, I heard the floorboards creaking just outside the half-open door in the hallway just at the top of the steps. This was not sledge-footed Big Guy. This was a light, almost dancing sound. Then, my mysterious guest bolted down the hallway toward the doorway with the sheet taped over its opening. As I ran to the corner of the room and looked down the hall, I saw the sheet jerk down. I knew whoever was in there was trapped, and I only had seconds before he would find that out. I raced down the hall into the pitch-black room. With my right arm, I hit the switch in an upward swing and prepared for a very serious encounter. With fists at the ready, I quickly surveyed the room. In the glowing ceiling, light only bemused piles of plaster, and lathe seemed to be hiding their imaginary mocking. My pulse was in my throat. I let down my fists and stood there running through each step of what I had just been through. It was no dream. The sheet was there on the floor where I had jumped over it. If I had run through it in some fantastic dream walk, it should have been carried further in the room. No, it was down, and I saw it come down. That was no crazy dream. It was reality, but what kind of reality? How did Mrs. Bowen live in this place? Then I thought about the sounds I heard. This was a different ghost. He was fast, sure-footed, and light on his feet. No stumbling oaf. So, I now had three ghosts. There was no other explanation. I suddenly felt drained of all energy. I turned out the light and walked down the hall toward the front bedroom door and the stairs to the left of the door. As I turned to cross the landing, I glanced up at the hall. Only the window and the empty wall. No ghost.

Years passed and my room that was created by the removal of the wall between the two middle rooms was finished. The windows on the south end of the room had been closed off, and a mural of fanciful jungle growth was painted on the solid wall. The windows on the opposite side would cast light into the room both day and night. There were odd sounds that continued to vex both the staff and me, but there had been no major incidents that left anyone shaking in their boots. That was until without warning I saw the fellow I had heard running down the hall into the closed off room.

At the end of the day, as the assistants were cleaning up rooms and closing out the accounts, I was going through the office turning off the many machines and lights. I was on the second floor and about to turn off the light in the lab. There are two sets of saloon doors to the tiny lab at one end of the space. I heard the same dance-like footfalls I had heard before, when I was taking out the wall between the two middle rooms. As I looked toward the sound, I saw under the far set of doors the legs of a very small man. He was prancing as he came toward me. Then he made a turn to his left and pranced right through a refrigerator that was on the other side of the wall and out of my line of sight. He wore russet-colored baggy knickers that had their cuff ends tightly folded into high-topped leather shoes that were laced up to mid-shin. I did not see the upper half of the little fellow because the saloon doors blocked my view. Just that fast, he danced right out of view, and I never saw him again. His outfit looked like what was worn in the 1880s by young men who were bicyclists. Perhaps he was getting ready to bicycle over to some young lady's abode. That was my impression. He seemed to either be unaware of me or did not care one way or the other. As I reflected on what I had seen, I assumed he did not exist in my time, but in his time. He might have been walking around the bed in his room as he made his way toward the wall where my refrigerator now existed but did not exist in his time. And so, right through the refrigerator he went. In an intersection of space and time, we were interacting in a common state of existence. I saw a young man repeating something he did about a century ago. I wonder if they see little vignettes of us doing things in what would be the future for them. So, our little moment between time and space came to an end, leaving me with so many questions. I stood there marveling at what I had just witnessed.

Much later, paranormal investigators would record on many occasions a happy little fellow who would scamper about the place and announce that he was Paco. Our Paco was a real joker, but I am getting ahead of myself.

10

Silent Touch and Invisible Tears

The sounds of Big Guy were heard by many people. My staff became afraid to go upstairs alone, especially when the sun went down in the winter months before the office closed. They had lockers that were for their coats, purses, and any snacks that they chose to bring to the office, but these items were all kept in the business office so that they could avoid going up to the second floor. When a task forced them to go up there, they arranged to go in pairs.

One of my Civil War reenactor friends called to ask if he could borrow a period coat from me to wear at some sort of a Civil War event that I was not able to attend. We arranged for him to pick up the coat just before closing as he was on his way to the event. He was a bit late arriving. The hygienist had left, and the receptionist had a previous engagement that required her to leave at about five o'clock, so when Mike entered the office, there was no one to greet him. He told me that while he was standing at the front desk, he heard someone walking around in the room just above him. Then it sounded like the person was dragging a very heavy piece of furniture across the room. He assumed I was up there doing some heavy work. He stepped into the hall and called up the stairwell for me and asked if I needed any help. All sounds stopped. He did not see anyone, and he did not hear me call back down to him as anyone would have expected. He debated whether or not he should check out the source of the odd noise.

As he was kicking these thoughts around, I, my patient, and assistant came out of the first operatory and made our way to the desk. I could see an odd expression on Mike's face, but he held his silence until after the patient had left. Then he told me what he had heard on the second floor. We went up the stairs and checked the whole place out. I assured him it was just one of our ghosts. Not to worry. Mike is one of those unflappable people who analyzes facts very quickly. He agreed that he had to have heard a ghost. He remarked on the incredible clarity of both the footfalls and the sounds of the heavy object that the ghost was dragging across the floor. I think he enjoyed the experience once he was certain that we had not made the noises. I have no doubt that what Mike described to have heard is exactly what he heard. He is one of those people who garner trust through long-standing relationships that are based on truth. I never knew him to betray that trust.

From the 1980s through the 1990s, the number of strange sounds steadily increased. Odd occurrences also escalated incrementally. We were hearing noises and feeling things brush past us with regularity. The employees reported the feeling as if someone was pulling at their hair as they worked at the front desk. These episodes were for the most part more puzzling than frightening. With the beginning of the millennium, the sounds became daily events. These minor disturbances were not recorded in our log, a book I had decided to start in which events were recorded as they happened with the writers putting down in their own writing what was experienced and signing and dating each entry.

At about that time, a change occurred in the way the entities that resided in the place manifested themselves other than the sounds and gentle touches. There were black shadow figures that appeared in the second-floor rooms. These were seen in the north-side rooms. Voices were heard, both male and female. This was new to us. Before, all sounds had been limited to physical noises of slamming doors, footfalls, and objects being moved in some way. The voices turned what was once almost amusing into something very disturbing.

One can always explain away the sound of a door slam, as just some noise from the outside that seemed to be inside the building. Voices, on the other hand, are intimate sounds that are right there with the listener. One such experience involved my cleaning service. The lady who cleaned the office at the time served my office and several other businesses in Huntington. On one occasion, Charlotte was upstairs working in the front bedroom area. When she entered the room, she heard the sounds of a child sobbing. She told me the sounds were deeply moving. They were the sounds of a young girl in terrific pain. She could not locate just where the sounds were coming from. They seemed to fill the whole room with the distant but very real cries of distress.

Charlotte's motherly instincts took over, and she sat down in a chair and began talking to the child as if they were actually together in the room. With a calming, reassuring voice, she told the ghost voice that she could hear her and that she was there to help her in any way she could. Charlotte told me she fully realized she was crossing the boundary between life and afterlife, but that did not frighten her. Her only concern was to find some way to comfort the poor child. Her own sense of pity overcame the shock of hearing the ghostly crying. Eventually, the sounds ebbed, and Charlotte was sitting alone in the room wondering what had just transpired between her and some entity from beyond the grave. She wondered what the poor thing was going through that would bring her to suffer so much even after death. She said the crying sounds haunted her for many months, and every time she entered the room, she spoke to the child reassuring her that she was not there to disturb her, and she wanted only to help her if she could

When my wife, Janet, and I were first married, she knew about the stories of hauntings in the office. At that time, they were, as far as she was concerned, just stories. Nothing would affect her. Or so she thought. The other thing she learned about the practice is that weekends are seldom spent entirely away from the office. I was, and still am, in and out of the place all weekend long, every weekend. On one such occasion, I had to stop by the office to pick up some papers that I had forgotten to bring home the day before. This stop would last only as long as it took me to get the papers from my desk and leave, but since the day was quite warm, Janet decided to go into the office with me. We had our little dog, Candy, with us, and so the three of us got out of the car and into the office we went.

I started up the stairs ahead of Candy and Janet and was just about to enter the front room, which was now my private office, when I heard Candy growling ferociously. I whirled around and looked over the railing to see what was going on. Candy was on the first flight of steps nearly to the top step. She was staring up at something she could see on the landing. The hackles on her back arched up like the hump on a buffalo. She lowered her eyelids and bared her teeth in the most aggressive expression I have ever seen in any animal. As I leaned over the railing observing her, I kept looking for what she was seeing that I could not see. Something was there. I decided Candy could see Big Guy! From deep inside her body came a throaty growl that gave voice to her intention to engage in mortal combat if her antagonist approached. Apparently, he did not move back as Candy had hoped he would do. Janet stopped in her tracks and was watching this unsettling transformation in our generally happy little dog. We both spoke to Candy asking in vain what was wrong. She ignored us entirely. I knew Janet could not see anything on the landing either since she was asking Candy what was wrong, just as I was. Then Candy surprised both of us. With hackles still up, teeth still bared, and that guttural growl still vibrating in her small frame, she began slowly backing down the steps. She never took her eyes from whatever she could see on the landing. She backed right into Janet's feet. Quickly turning away from the stairwell, Candy made a beeline for the door. She began frantically scratching to get out. Janet was in close pursuit, and out of the office they went. Seeing their unceremonious leave-taking and finding myself alone with whatever it was on the landing, I assumed it might still be there. Having total success with two of the three of us, it might try more direct tactics on me. At first, I thought of going through the long room to the hallway and the other stairwell and making my way down those stairs and out the door. Then I had second thoughts.

I descended the stairs with an air of unconcern. Humming a happy little tune, I crossed the landing and descended the flight of steps that Candy had backed down. My plan was to show this thing, whatever it was, that it did not have me in the grip of fear. I made it without incident. I found Janet and Candy having a stroll along the sidewalk. We joined up and I asked her how Candy was doing. Janet said that as soon as Candy was outside the building, she reverted to her old self. We discussed what it might have been. My guess, as I told her, was that Big Guy likes to frighten helpless little dogs. My lack of reaction in the stairwell to Big Guy may have helped me years later when I would have a planned confrontation with Big Guy. I often wondered if he was in the stairwell when I passed through it, or if he had already left that area having frightened my dog and my wife.

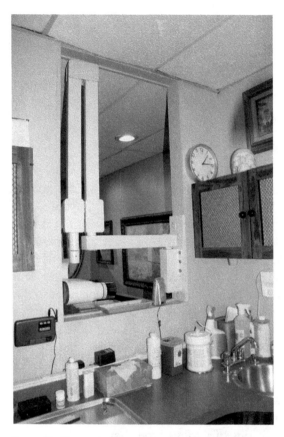

Figure 7: X-ray window with support arm that blocked the view of the face of the ghost in the room beyond. She moved rapidly to the left, disappeared behind the wall and began moving instruments, causing a clanging noise.

81

11

The Cast List Increases, Mysterious Lady

One of my assistants, Betty, was coming through the hallway from the first operatory and heading toward the waiting room on a typical morning in the middle of the work week. She saw some movement on the upper flight of steps. As she stopped to look, she could make out a black form, like a shadow of a tall man with his hands on the railing. He was leaning over the railing and appeared to be looking right at her. There were no visible features or details about the image. It was just a well-defined black shadow. She stood and watched as the shadow pulled back and disappeared from view. It made no sound. For that reason, I did not think it was Big Guy when she told us what she saw. This was one of the many observations recorded in our Ghost Log Book.

Different visions of various types began to make their presence known in the office on a fairly regular basis. We would see them about as often as we had heard them in the past. Between the two types of encounters, the employees began to tally which appeared most frequently.

As I was crossing the parking lot in the back of the building, I was making an assessment of what I could see of the outside. I always looked around the building in case there might be something that required attention. This is always a concern since on any given day or night, someone can damage or deface the office in a matter of seconds. I glanced upward to the two second-story windows at the back of the building and came face-to-face with a woman standing in the right window looking down at me. I had never seen her before. She had jet-black hair that was pulled back from her face and tied up in a bun. Her face was very pale. She was of medium build. Her eyes were dark brown like Lavina's. If she had any makeup on her face, I could not discern it from where I stood. She was wearing a simple white blouse that could have been from just about any decade after the dawn of the twentieth century. As I watched her, she seemed to become transparent. At the same time, she stepped back from the window and was gone. Now the list of apparitions was growing. At that time, I only knew one by name for certain. I wondered, who were the others? Were any of them related in any way, or were they simply arriving at the office through a portal that had opened up somewhere in the building?

A teacher friend of Janet's related a story at about the times she visited her grandmother who lived on one side of the duplex. When there, she often had dreams of people in late-nineteenth-century dress, standing around in the room. This would have been shortly before I purchased the property. The dreams might have been coincidental to the stories of the 1950s and the events I was involved with. There may have been no paranormal activity going on at all, and the young woman did not indicate that she thought she was dreaming about ghosts, but she always wondered what the meaning of the dreams might be. Could it be that, somehow, she was witness to the arrival of some of the entities through a portal that had just opened? She said they were just standing around. That could be what occurs when ghosts see an opportunity to enter into the realm of the living and once there, find themselves at a loss as to what they should do once they are there. (Another possible answer for her dreams is that her mind was trying to recreate a scene from a program she had enjoyed on television.)

One thing about portals I feel is certain. They do exist, and spirits do find a way to enter our time. This might explain the increase in involvement of spirits in the office. Or perhaps my work on the building caused them to suddenly come out of the places they were residing in to see what all the noise was about; like people in a motel being disturbed by some really loud sound in the middle of the night, causing them to get up from their beds to see what is going on. I am no expert in paranormal activity, so theories of my own making are nothing more than guesses. Whatever the cause for the increase in activity, we were certainly having a lot of it, by a lot of new characters.

It was October of 2002. I was working in operatory 2, with Karen assisting. We were not engaged in conversation at that particular time. The only sounds were those of the dental instruments and the classical music that was at a volume just high enough to be heard. Our patient was almost asleep. I became aware that someone was standing behind me as I sat on my operator's stool to the right of the patient. Karen looked up briefly, and thinking the person behind me was Betty, she asked what she wanted. There was no sound from the person behind me. No response of any kind. She just stood there behind me. Karen glanced up a second time asking what it was that she wanted.

At that instant, I felt a strange sensation of static electricity. It was building up very quickly and began to envelope me. A shudder went through me as if heat were being pulled out of me through my back. I swiveled my stool to the right. I could feel something pulling away from me. She was moving very rapidly through the open door and across operatory 1 toward the door that led to the downstairs hallway. That door was not standing open as was the door to operatory 2 where we were working, but she went right through it and disappeared. We could hear her as she ran through operatory 1. I never saw her because the direction in which I rotated my stool prevented me from facing her as she ran away. My back was to her the entire time she was with us. By the time I had rotated completely around to be able to see her, she was gone. I did not just turn my head as I rotated the stool because I had a drill in my right hand, which I had to transfer to my left hand as I turned to my right. I did not want the instrument to bang into the patient as I turned away from him.

Karen jumped from her stool and stood looking through the x-ray window that is in the wall between the two rooms. This way, the x-ray machine can be shared by both rooms. The dental chairs face away from each other with the x-ray directly behind each chair. "Where did she go?" asked Karen half to herself and somewhat to the patient and me. By that time, I had figured out what had happened. It was a ghost, not a person, who was standing behind me for a considerable amount of time. She was no more than six inches from my back.

Karen was certain beyond any doubt that the receptionist, Betty, had stepped into the operatory and for some reason, left in a hurry without letting us know what she wanted. Often, the assistant who is working at the reception area will come into the operatory where I am working to ask a question or to hand me a message. All assistants are trained to handle both positions so that substitutions can be made if anyone needs to be out of the office. It is not unusual for the front-desk person to come back, for many reasons, to where I am working. The odd thing for Karen was why Betty had not responded and then bolted from the room, running of all things! This they were trained not to do. She was not holding a chart. When there is a question involving a patient, the assistant at the front desk brings the chart and folder to me so that I can see who she is asking about without using names. I can also see treatments that have been completed and those yet to be done at a glance. This can all be accomplished without our current patient being aware of who or what we are addressing. All of this was skipped, and that was what tipped me off to the nature of the visitor behind me.

For Karen, the visit was another matter altogether. She was surefire certain Betty had been there behind me, and it was Betty who had some explaining to do. When Karen glanced up at the ghost, she saw long grayish-blond hair and assumed the woman was Betty. Later as we discussed the incident, Karen was certain that Betty was standing there and that she had on a crimson smock that had sleeves that were puffed at the shoulders. No amount of persuasion would make Karen think otherwise. "All right! I'll settle this!" she said as she marched out to the front desk. She asked Betty why she had entered operatory 2 and said nothing and then run out of there. Betty had not left the desk during that time and asked Karen what she was getting at. By the time I had made it to the front desk, Karen and Betty were sparring with what was turning into a very amusing debate.

Betty had the trump card. She took from the hook on the door her smock—an all-white smock. No puffy shoulders, no crimson color. There were no patients in the waiting room. It was not possible that someone who came with the patient had entered the operatory and left to return to the waiting room. That would be a very strange thing for anyone not employed with the office to do anyway. At any rate, there was no one in the office wearing the mysterious red smock Karen had seen. All the assistants had crimson scrubs, but there were no red smocks and no puffy sleeves.

I kept telling Karen she had seen a ghost, but that explanation of the situation was totally unacceptable to her. I was reminded of my father and how he had trouble accepting any suggestion that he had experienced a ghost. Karen kept insisting that she clearly saw sleeves that puffed at the upper areas. I came up with an idea. Waitresses used to wear uniforms with sleeves like that and usually an apron over the blouse. The apron was removed when the waitress left the business. Perhaps the ghost Karen saw had been a waitress in life and was wearing her work clothes when she came into the operatory. I told her that Lavina's mother and older sister were waitresses. Karen did not like my explanation. She suggested that we just drop the subject. It was not until several years had passed that Karen came to grips with the fact that she had seen and talked to a ghost.

Several years later, Karen would have another encounter that would leave her literally knocked to her knees.

In October 2004, I was with a patient in room 2. The patient had a very bad back and was not able to allow the dental chair to be tilted back very far. For this reason, I was standing beside her as we proceeded with her treatment. I had taken an x-ray and sent the chairside assistant, Rita, to develop the film in a processing machine that was located in the hygiene room. I was standing beside the patient and, at the moment, facing her as we engaged in pleasantries while waiting for the assistant to return the film to me. Through the opening in the wall through which the x-ray machine was operated, I could see into the other operatory to some extent. Something in operatory 1 caught my eye. I looked in that direction and saw whom I thought was Rita. My mistake was the result of my not being able to see the woman's face. The arm of the x-ray machine was right in the way. I could see, however, the top of her head and from her chin down to her waist. She was standing perfectly still with her hands clasped in front of her. Her hair was very similar to Rita's, a gray-blond color and falling straight to her shoulders. The illusion was completed by the color of her blouse, a pale olive green that was very similar to the color of the scrubs Rita was wearing. I was sure I was looking at Rita.

I asked her if she had my film. There was no answer or even acknowledgment that she had heard my question. This puzzled me. I repeated my question. No reply. I made a move toward the window and asked again if she had my film. As I drew close to the window, she moved very quickly to her right. Something about the way she moved alerted me that something was amiss. She moved as if she were on a conveyer belt. She scooted out of my line of sight at great speed. That was the moment I knew that I was looking at a ghost. Nothing about the thing was natural. She shot to my left and was out of my line of sight behind the solid portion of the wall. She began to rattle instruments that were lying on the countertop. As quickly as I was able, I changed my direction away from the window and toward the door to my left. Through the door, I glanced to my right expecting to see an apparition standing no more than three feet from me, but she had vanished.

I reentered the room with my patient calmly sitting there in innocent oblivion. I asked her if she had heard someone in the room behind her. She did hear the assistant I had apparently been talking to, and she was doing something with instruments. She had assumed the assistant was not the one I had been expecting to bring me the x-ray film since she seemed to be doing something unrelated. I thought that was an understatement. Whomever she was, she was not interested in my x-ray. The fact that my patient had heard the rattle of instruments validated what I experienced at the same time.

"Guess what? That was not an assistant. That was a ghost!" I said.

"Oh shoot!" she said. "Why didn't you tell me? I would have jumped up and finally seen a ghost!"

"Sorry, but there was no time. Besides, I didn't know myself until I saw her move away from the window and behind the wall where I couldn't see her," I replied. I told her what I saw and reiterated what she had heard.

I had assumed the apparition was Rita because of the similarity between the two. Rita and the ghost had light-colored hair with streaks of gray all through it. Both had hair that hung straight and was shoulder length, and both were wearing tops of the same color, a type of light olive green. In addition, the alignment of the x-ray arm blocked my view of the ghost's face. All these similarities and the fact that I was not able to see the face of the ghost resulted in my confusion. Even when she turned and moved beyond line of sight, the arm continued to hide her face until I approached the window. Then for an instant, I could see her face in profile. That was when I knew she was not Rita. Her face was pale. In fact, everything about her was muted in color. She looked like an image on a film processed in half tone. The amazing speed she possessed when she moved out of sight still amazes me.

She had a sad countenance but was determined to get something accomplished. She was very intent on whatever she had to do. I wondered if she even knew that I was asking her questions. If she did, she made no answer or even recognized my efforts to communicate with her. She may have been totally unaware that I was even there. And yet she handled instruments on the counter. Or was she in her own time getting ready to set the dining room table? Those amazing steps she made. They were smooth direct vectors of force. They were not the up-and-down movements of a live person walking. It was more like the flit of a housefly as it quickly darts from a resting position into flight. All was done in one smooth motion, too quick to see the change occur. It was inhuman in nature. My patient was not at all frightened in spite of the fact that I had just informed her that I had been talking to a ghost not six feet behind her. We had discussed ghosts on many occasions, and she often told me that she would love to see one. I told her, "Well, at least you got to hear one!"

12

Messages and Investigations

There is one episode that stands out in my mind, partly because of its uniqueness, and partly because it indicates that some ghosts possess a great deal of energy, or strength, as it were, and others are shy, happy, or melancholic in nature. Then there are those that are just bad. In my office, I encountered people with examples of each trait and ghosts of each trait. So, what I learned is that ghosts are just people who are without their bodies. That is all. Nothing complicated.

On December 20, 2005, as I crossed the waiting room headed to the business office, I noticed a heavy book standing out from its fellows on the shelves of the bookcase which provides reading material for our patients. For many years, I have had books in my waiting room rather than the usual magazines. They are all kept in a single bookcase. They cover a wide range of subjects, and each one is well illustrated with magnificent photographs. They go by the popular name of coffee table books. Patients like them because, unlike magazines, they have no annoying advertisements. My patients enjoy hunting for books on their favorite subjects in this small library.

On this particular day, there was that book standing out about five inches from the line of books on the shelf. The book was the heaviest book in the collection. It is exceptionally large and heavy and deals with the works of Michelangelo. What made the position of the book even more difficult to explain was the adhesion this particular book has when pushed back on the shelf with the other books. The jacket develops a static charge that causes it to be difficult to move.

As I pushed it back on the shelf, I noted the resistance of the book to movement in either direction. I asked Betty if she noticed the book standing out when she walked through the waiting room. She was in the business office at the time. She leaned out over the desk and high counter above it and assured me that it was not standing out. Since that put the book right in the way of anyone passing through the waiting room toward the office, she would have certainly seen it. I went into the office enclosure to gather the stack of patient charts for the day and jokingly remarked that our ghosts must be improving their cultural faculties. Betty said she hoped they would not start doing that all day. She had too much work to do.

After leaving the business office and rounding the corner of the enclosure, I stopped in my tracks. There in the waiting room in front of me was the same book standing out, only this time, it was even farther away from the other books. I called to Betty to step around and look at the book.

"That book is kind of hard to pull out," she said. "Someone is having some fun with us," I added. We were the only living people in the building. Office hours were not to start for another half hour.

Much later, I thought about the book incident, and it occurred to me that perhaps one of the ghosts was doing something other than having fun. This could be a demonstration of strength, a form of threat. The one who was pulling that book from the shelf might be demonstrating his ability. If he could do that, he could push someone into harm's way, down stairs or against something sharp. An ankle could be grabbed on a stairwell, causing a fall. If anything like that started happening, the office could be in for some real trouble. As it turned out, my assistant, Becky, did have an unexplained fall on the south-side stairwell that she insists was highly unusual. She found herself thumping against the stairs before she was even aware that she had fallen. After mentally going over and over her fall, she does not remember tripping or slipping. All she can recall is a rapid acceleration of her entire body toward the steps. It could have been an accident, but on the other hand, it could have been the result of Big Guy trying out ways to exert his energies onto us in a direct way to cause injury. I saw several doors swing shut with enough force to bang when they closed. I would think that it would take a great deal of effort for a spirit to accomplish something like that. Up to that point, I was willing to pass off the accidents and noises, but confrontation with a ghost in a way that resulted in personal injury was something I never really considered as a possibility.

I had been keeping a log of many of the events we experienced in the office. I tried to get all entries entered into the log as quickly as possible after each event had taken place. This way, details were less likely to be diminished by time. Simple episodes of hearing noises like bumps and creaks were not considered worthy of entry. Only really unexplainable occurrences were to be put in our Ghost Log. There were plenty of other experiences to enter, such as cold hands placed on shoulders, black shadows moving through the rooms, or outright full-fledged apparitions standing in a room. Even with this bit of editing, there were enough entries to fill up many pages. Our first paranormal group, Huntington Paranormal Investigations and Research, visited the office on May 4, 2007. They were at the office at 6:30 PM, and after introductions, I took them on a tour of the office, showing them where the events with our ghosts had occurred. I only covered the highlights; otherwise, the tour would have lasted several hours. They set up a base station in the waiting room and placed satellite cameras and microphones all over the office in rooms where they expected to pick up and record activity either of audible or visual nature.

When I returned to the office the following morning, they asked me if fragrances had ever been part of the experiences that anyone previously reported. I was surprised by this question. I had never even thought of the sense of smell coming into the picture as an indication of a haunting. As it turned out, several of the female investigators were in the room where Lavina died, trying to establish some type of communication with her or any other entity who might be there with her. They were hoping to record her voice answering questions they asked of her. Instead of a verbal communication, they were inundated with the dense sweet smell of a peach perfume. They all responded to it at the same time, and each agreed that it was a peach perfume or scent that they experienced. They told me that female ghosts often produce scents like that. It is their way of saying that they are present and want to extend greetings and friendship. They explained to me how their investigation was conducted, and the function of the various devices besides microphones and cameras. EMF monitors respond to electromagnetic fields. Once areas of naturally occurring electromagnetic fields are mapped out in all areas of investigation, the team looks for variations in these fields to determine paranormal activity.

Ghosts seldom emit sounds that can be recognized as voices. They are more likely to use their energy to alter electronic devices in a way that produces an accurate recording of their voices. The investigators seldom hear voices during their investigations. Not until they play back the recordings they made during their time at a place of interest do they pick up these electronic voice prints, or EVPs. As questions from the investigators become answered on the recordings, the investigators label them "intelligent hauntings." The term for responses that cannot be recorded, such as the odor of peach perfume, comes under the heading of "personal experience." Into this category would fall touching sensations, responses to cold, and even the sense of depression and of nausea.

On June 25, 2007, we met with the team to see and hear what they had found as tangible evidence of haunting. In addition to the story of the odor, they had three recordings that were of the EVP type since there were no audible sounds associated with the voices that were recorded. The first was the sound of a whimpering child. This recording was made at the top of the north-side stairwell. For me, this was an important connection to the little girl, Lavina. I listened to the recording several times. It was an unmistakable whimpering sound, and it sounded like a little girl. The other recordings were picked up at the foot of the same stairwell. One was definitely an adult male coming across loud and clear. "Garth," was all that was said.

Another strong male voice said, "Bus." There was no doubt that the recordings were human voice sounds and not some noise made by a mechanical means. What could one make of just two words? What was to be made of them? We had no idea. There was just not enough to go on.

Much later, a person who claimed to be a sensitive said she got the impression that Garth was not a person but a cat. Oddly enough, I had found the skeleton of a cat in the crawl space under the building. I picked up the skull and started going over the anatomical landmarks that I had learned in a comparative anatomy class while attending Marshall University. On a whim, I put the skull in my pocket and put it on the wall in my lab after disinfecting it thoroughly. It was a male cat. Could it be Garth? I decided to name the skull, Garth, and so Garth it remains to this day.

In 1953, a grandmother was walking her two grand-daughters to the bus stop on Charleston Avenue. When they arrived at the area in front of the duplex that later became my office, she pointed to the house and said, "Now that's the house that's haunted." Could the word *bus* refer to this story of the two girls and their grandmother? That is anyone's guess.

Then again, we may have only recorded one word from two sentences uttered by someone who was relating a completely different subject than cats, and girls on their way to catch a bus. Later I took the CD with the recordings, which the paranormal group had given to me, to my daughter's home. She had equipment that was much more sensitive than any I had. On her device, we could hear distinctly the sound of a little girl saying, "Mommy," rather than whimpering as we had thought we had heard when listening to the recording on the equipment the researchers used. This was more meaningful for me since it was a word, and it was the voice of a female child. The voice had a disturbing sound of fear to it. I wondered if it was Lavina reacting to the strangers in her home with all their equipment, which does look a bit frightening.

13

What Dogs Know

The claw-foot bathtub on the north side had been removed long ago by my father and me. This allowed space for the furnace unit to be placed on the second floor rather than to take up valuable space on the first. I decided to leave the twin tub on the south side where there would be space on the first floor for an additional furnace unit. The unit on the south side would have walls built around it, forming its own little furnace room. This was done in the dining room on that side, and the hygienist operatory was built into the remaining area. This one remaining bathtub afforded a magnificent spa quality bathing facility for our three rescue dogs. We enjoy treating them to a grandiose canine resort-style retreat of their very own.

In July of 2007, one of our little loved ones was out of the porcelain spa taking his usual victory romp through the upstairs rooms. The long room that allows easy access from one side of the duplex to the other on the second floor is one of the favorite areas for the dogs to run around in circles celebrating their baths. One little fellow ran through that room and down the north side hall toward the north stairwell. Something caught his attention down in the stairwell. He stopped his frenzied romp and for a few seconds, cocked his head as he looked into the darkness of the unlighted area. Then he began barking. I was in the hallway right behind him, watching. The barking became more intent for about thirty seconds, and then he became silent. He raised his ears and cocked his head again as if trying to decide what or whom he was looking at. Then he began barking and growling at something down on the first floor. I was listening very intently and watching everything Angus did.

To my surprise, he suddenly stopped acting as if there was an intruder in the hallway below and casually walked past me, turned the corner, and entered the long room as if nothing had happened. I stood there in the dark hall peering into the darkness of the stairwell. I did not sense anyone's presence. I took a few quiet steps toward the light switch and turned it on, looking for any sign of a person down there. There was none. I concluded Angus had heard a ghost, figured this out, and decided it was not a threat to either of us. During the entire event, he did not once look at me. He did it all on his own. When I went back down the hall after turning out the light, there was Angus sitting on the floor at the far end of the room calmly waiting to be leashed up for his trip back home.

Since he did not react to the ghost the way Candy had done years before on the same stairwell, I concluded he did not see anything. He was reacting to sounds only, or if he did see a ghost as well as heard it, the ghost might not have posed a threat as had the one Candy saw. Either way, his encounter had him going for a time and then ceased to be a concern for whatever reason. With Angus leashed up and by my side, we checked out the whole office, turning on lights as we entered every room, and turning all of them off when we left. He walked with me in complete calm. Whatever it was, he did not experience it a second time.

Now I had two incidents involving dogs in the same stairwell. When one analyzes the two situations, certain conclusions can be made. First, the dogs were reacting to something they truly perceived to be real. In the first case, the intensity of threat caused the dog to retreat. In the second case, something defused the threat, and the dog simply settled down and calmly walked away. In that one difference, there are several possible causes. The similarity lies in the discovery of some being in the stairwell. No matter the difference of how the two events ended, the discovery of something there is the key. Dogs do not make things up. They do not tell lies. Unlike people, they are very good witnesses. In these two events, the dogs were truly believable. A human reacts to a disturbing stimulus with bias, cultural influences, and presumptive attitudes. It would be difficult to describe dogs as having these obstacles to objectivity when thrust into an encounter with a thing that could not be understood from past experiences. For that reason, I believe dogs are better witnesses than we are. Beyond this, we do not train our dogs in any way other than routine house training. They are not trained to do any tricks, or to guard, defend, and protect us in any way. We prefer that our pets be themselves and not creatures of our own egos. They reacted in both cases on their own.

101

14

Shadows and ToiletPaper

By 2008, sightings and sounds had increased. In earlier periods such activity was on a bimonthly basis, relatively speaking. Now encounters were reaching weekly to biweekly average. During October of 2008, Betty was working not only as an assistant but also was working after hours cleaning the office. She reported seeing and hearing more unexplainable things than we were experiencing during office hours. The same was true for me. I found myself having to spend a lot of time in the office on weekends doing repairs and changing the decor of many rooms. In the silent rooms, the only sounds I heard were those I made myself. Then when I least expected it, some sound would have me looking around for an intruder. When I checked the place out and found nothing alive had caused the noise, I was always greatly relieved. Betty reported on several occasions seeing black shadows that flitted through the rooms at great speed. I saw the black things on two occasions myself. During this time, we had many paranormal investigations, and these people saw on several occasions the same black shadows pass right by them. One was caught on video during one such investigation. Then another shadow was recorded, but in the recording from an infrared camera, the shadow shows up as white, not black. This means to me that the two recorded shadows are of different substances. How could one be black and the other white unless there was some material difference in the two? The recorded black shadow was picked up in the back room on the north side, while the recorded white shadow is seen crossing the north end of the long room. There is also a difference in the rate of speed between the two. The black shadow moved extremely fast, while the one that shows up as white moves at a much slower pace. It moves about as fast as a person walking in haste, just below what would be a jogging speed.

Julia worked in the office at the front desk for a number of years. A retired teacher, she never met a stranger. She was anything but a wallflower. Her solid, positive personality and sense of humor made everyone around the desk want to join in on every conversation in which she was engaged. At the same time, she could switch gears and soothe those patients who were in pain. This balancing act went on all day every day. On one occasion, she witnessed something that was unique, strange, chilling, and funny too. Julia was in the women's restroom, tidying up the area, when a motion caught her eye. The wall-mounted roll of toilet paper was unrolling. It was turning on its own. The loose end went down to the floor and began piling up as the roll continued to rotate. She said she stood there watching it in total amazement. One might think this would be easy to explain, except for one detail. The cardboard tube was flattened into a sharp oval. It was not round. Julia watched it go bump. Bump. Bump. As the oval-shaped tube thumped on the supporting bracket. In her typical way, she described what she saw as the "little roll that could." Julia brought me to see the roll and described what had just taken place. At first, I did not realize what she had seen. I assumed she had just entered and found the toilet paper in the condition she had found it in. To me, there was no reason to be excited about that. I was about to turn and leave when she said, "No, I watched it unroll on its own!" She spoke slowly and emphasized each word. That is an old teacher's trick to make a student follow her train of thought. It worked. Finally I understood what she was trying to get me to understand. I fiddled with the roll and came to the conclusion that it could not unroll on its own. "Wow!" I said half to her and half to myself. "Do you suspect ghosts go to the bathroom?" Julia smiled and, raising her hands in resignation, told me that she didn't have a clue.

April of 2008 was a time when we had an encounter that really shook Betty even after all she had seen and heard up to that time. We were working on a patient's denture that needed repair of a crack that divided it into two halves and left several teeth broken loose. The patient was quietly sitting in the dental chair with his bib on. I was turned away from him facing the counter that was behind him. I had covered all the details of what I was going to do with the denture so that the patient would be clear about the procedure. It was now just a matter of getting the job done. The only problem was that we were pressed for time. I was already fifty minutes behind schedule. Our lunch hour would be very late, if at all—unless I could accomplish the repair in record time.

As I began the task, I saw in my peripheral vision a woman with black hair watching me through the x-ray window. She was standing there in the other operatory looking at me. Then she leaned forward for a better look at what I was doing. I assumed Becky had entered operatory 2 through the passageway in that room that connected it with the other side of the building. She often used that door to gain access to the operatories because it was a more direct path from the front desk. I assumed she could see what I was doing and made a mental calculation of how long it should take me to finish the repair. When we are late releasing a patient, Becky often ventures to the operatory where we are working so that she has some idea how to best do her job at the front desk. Sometimes she will discuss with me her situation out front, and I then describe what we are up to with our end of the process.

In this case, I assumed she could easily see just what was going on since the broken denture was in plain view. Then everything changed. The black-haired woman suddenly moved away from the window. At that moment, Betty rose from her assistant's stool and quickly stepped toward the door of room 2. It was at that moment that it dawned on me that something was not right. That feeling of static electricity crept up my spine, and I realized that I probably had not seen Becky after all.

I began running through the last few minutes in my mind and realized that before seeing the woman in the x-ray window, the light in that room dimmed. The sense of static electricity was going on when I first saw her, but I had ignored it because I was intent on getting the repair complete before too much time had been lost. My determination to successfully conclude this goal had caused me to miss a very close face-to-face encounter with a ghost. She was about a yard from the tip of my nose. When Betty came back into the room, the surgical mask on her face did not conceal her shock. She sat down heavily on her stool with eyes wide open looking at me. She looked, well, like she had just seen a ghost.

"Was that what I think it was?" I asked. "Uh-huh," she replied vaguely.

After the patient was released, Betty told me what she saw. She was still in a state of shock and was speaking very slowly. She thought at first, as I had thought, that Becky had entered room 2 to check on the progress we were making, but when the ghost leaned forward, near the opening, Betty could see her directly and immediately knew that she was not Becky. She had dark-brown hair and a light-green blouse. She was watching me with an expression of incredulity, wondering why I was in her dining room working on some man's denture. At the moment she entered the room and was approaching the opening Betty and I noticed the room grow slightly dark, as if one of the ceiling lights had blown. Within a few seconds, the room returned to a normal level of illumination. At that time, she leaned over the countertop on her side of the wall and watched me working, and Betty could look straight at her. Betty then saw her abruptly pull away from the window and move to our right. That was when I broke my concentration on the denture and began to realize that Becky was not the one looking at me.

What I did not see was that she transformed into a black smoke-like cloud and vanished. Betty said that upon seeing that, she got up and went to the door of operatory 2 and looked around but saw no sign of the woman or a black shadow. I wondered if the black shadow seen so often on the second floor might be this woman. Could she represent herself in that way? Perhaps it would take less energy to take that form than the form of a full-figured solid apparition. One thing was certain, the black forms were more common than before.

The patient did not realize that anything of a supernatural phenomenon was transpiring right behind him as he sat there facing the opposite direction. He was elderly, and we had never discussed anything about the ghosts in the office with him, so we decided to keep him out of the loop. Many patients were put in this category. We often kept them out of the conversations we had after seeing things like what Betty and I had just seen.

Another episode with a shadow figure occurred in the back room on the second floor on the north side. That room was the center of nearly all the black apparition sightings and the one caught on a recording during an investigation. It was January 2009, a bright sunny day with low temperatures that never got above freezing. I was in the snack room. I had installed in that room a bank of three lockers for use by my assistants. I thought they would like to have a secure place for purses and coats. As it turned out, they learned to keep their coats in their cars and their purses with them downstairs. They didn't want to have to go upstairs for their things in a darkened snack room at the end of the day. (They use the lockers only for snack foods now.) I wanted a convenient place to hang some cleaning equipment in the snack room. The end of the array of lockers turned out to be the perfect place to put a hook to hang these items on.

From my position, I could see across the two saloon doors and into the back room on the other side. The saloon doors are located so that one set is in the snack room, and the other set is in the back room, with the lab extending along two solid walls between the two rooms. A motion caught my attention at the set of doors on the far side of the lab. I looked straight at a solid onyx-black object that looked like a very tall person completely draped in a black cloth. I would guess he, or it, was well over six feet tall. One hand was holding the top of one saloon door. The hand was not bare but was draped in the black material. For a few seconds, we stood there looking at each other. We were both frozen, standing perfectly still, as if wondering what to do next. Then, with a jerk backward, the thing moved very rapidly away, pulling the door with it as that one hand withdrew from the top edge. As it pulled back, it began to shrink until it was completely gone. It seemed to go into a small hole in the wall, as if it either entered the wall, or passed through it. There was only the sound that the saloon door made as its hinges creaked during the jerk of the hand off it.

I stood there in amazement for a full minute looking at the area where the thing once stood. I noticed that the bright light coming through the window on the far side had no effect on the black object. It was as black as any black I had ever seen. Onyx is the only way to accurately describe the black of the shadow. There was no transparency at all.

In fact, it seemed to be absorbing all light that fell upon it. It was wild and crazy, but for some reason, I was not frightened by it. I walked through the two sets of doors and looked around the room where the thing had been standing. There was no sign of it having been there. I went back into the snack room and, using the intercom, reported to the front desk what had just happened. I invited the two gals down there to come up and see where I was and where the black thing was. There were no takers.

15

Sixth Scents

By this time, I had become an unemotional observer of the phenomena I encountered in the office. My response to the things I had seen by that time evoked curiosity and a need to understand the nature of their physical properties. There was so much to learn.

I am notorious for my lack of a sense of smell. I will not notice many odors that assail my coworkers. They often marvel at the lack of response I display while they work with me. Health care is not a pretty job. We deal with infections of all kinds, and patients who have other problems that evoke nostril insults. I have a little bit of an ability to pick up on some things that perfume the air in varying ways, but not much.

Then, in January of 2009, I had a one-of-a-kind experience that still baffles me. I was descending the north stairwell returning to operatory 1, having just completed work in the lab on the second floor. When I came to the landing in the stairwell, I stepped into a virtual cloud of luxurious and wonderful smelling Smith Brothers Wild

Cherry cough drops. What a treat! I stopped dead in my tracks. The sweet smell of the wild cherry drops was so strong I could almost taste them. I stood there a minute enjoying the scent and remembering how I loved those cough drops as a child. Then I wondered how I was able to pick up on that scent. I checked around and found that it was only on the landing. I went to the lower hallway sniffing as I went, suspecting I would discover the source in the women's restroom, but to my surprise, it was not on the lower flight of stairs, or in the women's restroom. I returned to the landing, and there it was! It made my mouth water.

I remembered that my daughter, Carey, and one of her sons, Coby, were in the waiting room. I entered the waiting room and told them to follow me. I went to the landing. It was still there, but not as strong. I asked them if they smelled anything. Coby answered immediately that he smelled wild cherry candy. While we stood there, the scent evaporated and was no longer discoverable anywhere. We searched for a possible source in all the rooms. There was none anywhere. For me, to smell anything at all at such magnitude made the experience one I will never forget and one I will never understand. Why wild cherry? Who did that, and why? Like so many things that have happened in the office, there are no answers. (I really enjoyed it, however.)

On March 5, 2009, Carey's husband, Jason, and their two sons Kyle and Coby were on the second floor with me. I was demonstrating the EMF meter. We were walking around through the rooms as I held the meter. As we passed a saddle which is mounted on a wooden stand, I mentioned that Lavina often enjoys sitting on it. Sure enough, the EMF meter went wild when I came near the saddle. "There she is!" I exclaimed. As I held the meter above the saddle, I explained how the thing picks up on energy that ghosts are composed of, but not the electromagnetic field that we all possess. As I said that, Lavina got off the saddle and stood right in front of the two boys. As I went up and down with the meter, I demonstrated that she was right there, and I showed them how tall she was by holding the meter on the floor and slowly raising it until it stopped measuring a field in the area right in front of the boys. "She is this tall," I said, holding my hand as if it were on Lavina's head. The two boys were beginning to pick up on Lavina's presence. We played a bit with her and then returned to the first floor. I think they accepted the situation as it was. Their reaction was not one of fear but of curiosity that had been peaked through the experience.

March 28, 2009, marked the date of a turning point in the ghostly happenings at the office. A paranormal group operating under the name Mountain State Paranormal arrived and set up a phenomenal amount of equipment in the office. They were serious about capturing and recording as much evidence of a haunting in the place as possible. Once they were set up, I went out to my car in the parking lot and waited.

At about one o'clock in the morning, the two women on the team came out to the car to tell me about a very long session they had had with a little girl at the top of the stairs on the north side. A recording they played back after part of the session captured the voice of a little girl claiming to be named Robin. They used a flashlight which they placed on the floor between them as they sat on the floor at the top of the steps. The little girl would turn the light on and off in order to answer their questions, but she was reluctant to tell them what her name was. Robin was an alias we decided. They were absolutely charmed by the little girl. She was sweet and playful and clearly brought out the maternal instincts in the two investigators.

They then told me that they were going to break a rule by asking me to come inside and be present for the remainder of the session with the little girl who called herself Robin. I was told that the flashlight session they had had was the best by far than any they had ever experienced. They brought me to the top of the stairs, and we all sat down in the hallway. I watched as the flashlight was used by the ghost in response to the questions they asked. Finally, after somehow turning the light on and off for so many times, she became tired and was unable to get the light either all the way on or all the way off. The light would flicker as if it had a short in its switch. It was fascinating to see

As we sat together on the floor, we could feel her moving about. She seemed to be an energy field about the size of a beach ball. She floated over our laps and between us. We could feel a very cold sensation as she moved around us. It was as if some connection with the three of us had been made that erased the shyness. For the first time, she seemed to trust people enough to play with us as if she were a living child. I realized she had been more afraid of me than I was of her. On that night, a bond was formed between us. "Robin" rested against one of the women as she nestled on her lap. She told us that where the spirit touched her felt like a bolus of frigid air against her. Her jeans were indeed ice-cold. The three of us had an experience none of us will forget.

Several weeks after that, we were contacted by the two women, and we set up a time to meet for what the teams all call their Reveal. This is the session some paranormal groups will have with the owners of the places investigated and during which the data and recordings are revealed. In my case, there were about a dozen people who attended this reveal. They heard about it and asked to be there to see for themselves what was found by the team. The team went through the evidence on a computer screen. They showed us a video of the flashlight session and a vague image of a very large man descending the stairs. Sound recordings included a playful fellow who called himself Paco. He announced himself numerous times on several different recording machines. But the recording that really sent the mood of the reveal in an entirely different direction was one of the little girl saying, "He killed me."

There was no mistaking the voice. There was no mistaking the words either. We were all stunned. We had the team play the recording over and over. All that was left for us was to figure out if Lavina had died of natural causes as Mrs. Andre had been told back in 1929, or was there another explanation for her death? Did someone kill her accidentally, or was she murdered? Then again, were we jumping to conclusions thinking that we were communicating with Lavina in the first place? Did two girls die in the office, or had this spirit entered the same place Lavina had died after dying herself in some other location? For every one step forward, we seemed to take at least three back. Only one thing was certain, something happened in the office that was not good, and somehow that incident was causing the spirit of a young girl to try to get someone to understand what it was.

16

Making Friends with Lavina

Now I know why the ghost of the little girl had been appearing to me and communicating with an increasing number of paranormal investigators. The problem was that there was not enough to go on. We had a number of theories, and that was as far as we could go with what we had. For me, the transition from Lavina dying from an illness to something beyond that cause of death was not easy. For years, I was convinced that I knew exactly what had occurred. Suddenly I was given reason to doubt that information, but I was not able to let go of my conviction that Mrs. Andre was correct in her story. Finally, after much more information, I changed my mind.

This change in belief brought collateral changes that went in many different directions. The question of how Lavina really died became an obsession of mine. The only problem was that I lacked the time to work directly on finding answers. The other problem was that I had no idea how to launch an investigation. Then there was the doggedly perplexing possibility that the recording was a deliberate misdirection, started by a spirit that sounded like a little girl and wanted to play a joke from beyond the grave. If this was what was going on, I may have stumbled onto the ghost of Orson Welles! But I doubt it.

The paranormal team suggested that I should nurture my relationship with the ghost of the little girl whether or not she turned out to be Lavina. We were all convinced that the recordings suggested a genuine tragedy had occurred in the house I owned, and a very real ghost was indeed trying to convey the answer to the mystery of the tragedy. Using that premise as a starting point, I should establish a relationship that would enhance trust. By building upon that basic relationship, I might move on to establish a form of communication and open a door that had been closed for decades—an open door that would unlock the mystery.

At that time, the little girl seemed to be more open to females, so at the end of the reveal, the women who were present were invited to the top of the stairs for a session with the ghost, if she would allow it. Present were Carey, Julia, Becky, my hygienist Julie, and the two team investigators. As it turned out, she seemed more willing than ever to communicate with them. But when asked who she was, she answered, "Brittany." For some reason, she was still hiding from us. Lack of trust? Probably. When asked if she wanted anything the answer on the K-2 machine was, "Candy!" Further questions uncovered a specific type of candy was desired. Chocolate. With this information provided so willingly, someone asked if she would like to have toys. Dolls perhaps? The answer was, "Yes!" With that, we made plans to provide these items at the top of the stairs along the banister railing in the hallway. I decided to try a small box of chocolates and leave it on the floor with some toys. Betty came up with a splendid idea. She had some soft plastic letters and numbers that we could arrange to spell out messages on the floor along with the candy and toys. With the letters, I spelled out the word *candy* right next to the box of chocolates.

The next morning when I arrived at the office and went to the top of the stairs to the front room, where I change into my scrubs, I was stopped dead in my tracks. The *c* in candy had been moved and rotated toward the box of chocolates. The *y* had been rotated in place. The other letters appeared to be just where I had placed them the day before. One might claim that a mouse had tripped over the letters as it scurried around the chocolates; however, the box of chocolates was not disturbed, and the individual pieces were not so much as scratched. I do not think any self-respecting little critter would pass up the chance to at least see what filling was inside the chocolates. No, it had to be the little girl.

All in all, the team had recorded 127 EVPs, recorded the strange video of the outline of a very large man going down the north side stairwell and recorded a really mystifying video of an orb that was the size of a softball floating out of the front room to the upper hallway, and drifting down the hall toward the camera, disappearing as it floated above and beyond the camera, which was mounted on a tripod. At that time, there was no one around. The investigators told me that they dismiss orbs as evidence of paranormal activity, but there was something about this one that made it worth keeping with the rest of their evidence. On several occasions after this investigation, there were similar recordings of orbs much like the first one. They all seemed to be similar in form and size. They all left the front room and went down the hallway. Whether or not these orbs are spiritual in nature is anyone's guess, but I like to think they are the little girl, Lavina. By this time, I was convinced that Lavina was the identity of the ghost we called the Little Girl. I began talking to her when I found evidence that some entity was at the top of the stairs. I used my EMF meter often, and more often than not, there would be evidence that she was there.

I became fond of her. It was like a like a long-distance relationship between two people. She kept moving the toys from time to time. It was enough to let me know she enjoyed them, all except for two old-fashioned porcelain dolls placed there by one of our patients. Our patients were hearing stories about the ghost of a little girl at the office. Many of them brought toys for the child ghost. That was how the porcelain dolls arrived on the scene, brought there by a professional plumber, Jim. (More about him later.)

All these people giving Lavina gifts seemed to produce results by way of activity in every area of the office. There were many occasions involving sweet floral scents. Two of these occasions I enjoyed myself. The scent I received reminded me of the smell of honeysuckle. That is one blossom I can actually discern for some reason. Most other flowers just have an odor that I cannot separate from the general smell of a hospital, florist, or mortuary. On March 13, 2009, Betty, Julia, and I picked up on the same

119

scent of very sweet honeysuckle. It was very strong, even for my diminutive ability.

17

"Staff Meetings"

On April 30, 2009, Julia worked overtime into the evening to catch up on some of the paperwork that had been piling up in the business office. While at her workspace, she felt cold air at her back. It slowly surrounded her as if someone was embracing her as she sat there. She felt it come closer to her, and then it put its icy arms around her. She said it was frigid. She sat still wondering what would happen next. Slowly, she turned to see if there was some person actually behind her. She could see no one. She was alone with a ghost. As she turned the icy arms and chest quickly pulled back from her, and the cold sensation completely left her. The room felt perfectly normal again. She told us that there was no sound, no rustling of clothing, or footfalls. Only the icy embrace. It passed and that was that. Her chilling visitation from beyond the grave ended as completely as it started. She could not say if it was a man or a woman, but it seemed to mean no harm.

On June 6, 2009, Becky had been in operatory 1 discussing the planned treatment of a patient with me as I was working with another patient. She finished our discussion and left, going through the first-floor hallway and out into the waiting room. She was looking down as she turned the corner to walk through the waiting room and into the business office. Something caught her eye. She looked up and saw a little old woman at the far side of the L-shaped counter. The woman was looking straight at her. Assuming that someone had just entered the office, she asked if she could help the woman. At the same time, she was asking herself who the woman might be and how she got into the office without causing the door buzzer to sound while she was in operatory 1 with me. The front door sets off a buzzer to sound in the two operatories back where I work. Another buzzer is located upstairs in the lab. It can be heard in every room upstairs. As these questions were bouncing around in Becky's head, the little old woman vanished right before her eyes. This happened just as Becky was about to speak to her. Since the woman was short, Becky assumed she had sat down on the bench located at the far wall. If she did, she would have quickly dropped out of sight. When Becky reached the desk, she looked around it to the bench. It was empty. There was no one in the room. Becky took a quick turn to her right and entered the hygiene room where Julie was at work on her patient. Becky sat on a bench in Julie's room. After settling down a bit, they engaged in small talk. Even though she could not see anything in the office from where she sat, she decided against going back out there just then. For the rest of the day, she could not stay out in the business office area without someone else there with her. The sighting had really rattled her.

I told her I knew just how she felt. The first time you see a ghost, your ability to set the experience aside and go on with business as if nothing happened is not easy. I told her about the time I first saw Lavina at the top of the stairwell and how I ran out of the office. My reaction was a lot sillier than hers had been by a long shot. No one knows what they would do in that situation. Not until they come face-to-face with a real, honest-to-goodness, ghost, looking right at them

On July 22, 2009, Betty and I were treating a patient in operatory 2. Under the counter are two sets of drawers, and behind the assistant's position, there is a cabinet with a door that is kept closed by a strong magnetic catch. A small opening in the upper area of the cabinet door allows small items of trash to be placed inside without having to open the larger door. This opening has a trapdoor with a hinge along its top edge. The little trapdoor swings inward freely. Without warning, the larger door opened quickly and just as quickly slammed shut. It closed with such force that the small trapdoor swung back and forth several times. I was there to see this all happen. Betty had her back to it. I stopped working on my patient and sat there looking at the door. It all happened so fast. Betty looked at me and turned toward the door.

"What was that?" she asked. "I have no idea," I answered.

The patient heard the door slam after popping open and was, therefore, aware that something very odd had just occurred. We all discussed the episode for a few minutes while Betty opened and closed the door. The door catch does not allow the door to simply come open. One has to pull it open with a bit of a tug on the knob. One other thing is even more difficult to understand. The door slammed shut, yet there are no springs in the door to cause this to happen. If the door is opened, it will stand open until manually closed. Yet it closed with force. The only explanation we could agree on was that a ghost opened the door and closed it. Why? Perhaps to frighten us. If he tried to do that by opening and closing a door, he failed. None of us were even slightly afraid.

Figure 8: Armoire that has the ghost of a cranky old watch repairman attached to it.

18

Innocent Pranks or Intimidation?

The Proctorville Paranormal Investigating Team spent the night of July 30, 2009, in the office, having their try at finding out what was going on at 1125 Twentieth Street. I was contacted by the team early the next morning to say that they were ready for me to come to the office and lock the place up. I arrived much earlier than they expected. Seeing that they were far from completing their packing, I waited in my waiting room and watched as they scrambled all over the office, turning off various pieces of equipment, reeling up hundreds of feet of wire, and packing their equipment into black trunks and cases with aluminum strapping that was just like that used by sound technicians on a road show. They were all very excited about a large variety of personal experiences that they had encountered during the night.

As each member completed his task, he joined his fellows in the waiting room with me. Two young men told me about an incident they witnessed while they were in the room in which Lavina had died. They placed an electromagnetic field monitor on the floor in the hallway at the top of the stairs. They were trying to communicate with Lavina or her mother in the room without having any luck. Then they heard the sound of someone ascending the stairs. They were certain another investigator in their team was headed toward them. When the footfalls seemed to be at the top of the stairs, the meter went ballistic. Then the meter shut down, and there were no sounds. One of the two men turned his flashlight to the door opening and found that there was no one there. This all made the two men ecstatic. They couldn't stop talking about their encounter. I told them that the ghost we call Big Guy was most likely responsible for the sounds, and that he went up and down the stairs a lot. They told me that made sense, because the sounds were those of a very heavy man.

In the waiting room, I have a collection of items from Huntington's past. Among the items is a trunk of open slats that once contained farm produce on the paddle steamers that plied the waters of the Ohio River in the days when steam was king of transportation. One of the team members placed his EMF meter on the trunk. He had not turned it off. While we were talking, the meter suddenly went into active mode. Everyone became quiet, and he turned his attention to the meter. It was pegged at maximum response. The young man picked it up and began to move it in arcs around the area where it first came on. It would increase and decrease in a space about the size of a person sitting on the floor in front of us. Another investigator turned on a recorder and began asking questions. We did not get any responses to any questions, and after about ten minutes, the entity seemed to rise up and leave the area. That is the way it often goes when contact is made to communicate with the spirit using other devices. What is going on is anyone's guess. Often the spirits do not want to make any contact with us other than to tell us to leave the area. It is all very strange.

During that night, I was told that one investigator had to leave the building because of a severe headache. He sat outside in his car, and the headache went away in about ten minutes. Since he thought he was over with it, he reentered the office and tried to resume his task, but the longer he stayed inside, the more severe his headache became for a second time. He left again. As the team was breaking down their equipment, the young man returned and told me about his headache trouble. He might have been reacting to some substance used within the office, but he thought it odd that after several hours on the first floor without a headache, he had one flare up on the second floor two times. We use a lot of chemicals on the first floor for dental procedures, and for sterilization purposes, but only household items typical to any home are used on the second floor. The headaches started after the team member had spent time on the second floor. He was not affected while on the first floor. That was odd, but not conclusive that he was affected by some paranormal force. We all decided to not try to make too much of it. Having said that, such reactions are common among people who are directly confronting spirits in a place known to have high incidence of activity. Many researchers over the years had similar problems while investigating my office. Whether these reactions are evidence of paranormal influence or just emotionally generated flights of imagination, one cannot say.

127

Late in the year 2009, there were some funny things that happened in operatory 3, the hygiene room. Penny was cleaning the office at that time, in addition to working in the position of dental assistant, and she had numerous incidents in which the spirits seemed to be playing pranks on her. Most of these practical jokes occurred in the hygiene room. She always left the rooms in perfect condition with no detail left unnoticed or not taken care of. On one evening, when she was trying to get home for a football game on television, some ghostly prankster was set on delaying her. Each time she left the hygiene room and reentered, she was greeted by a jumbled mess of boxes of gloves, tissues, and miscellaneous items scattered helter-skelter all over the countertop. The first few times she saw this happen she doubted her memory. Surely, she had not forgotten to straighten everything with precision before leaving the room. Then time and time again, she found things in total disarray.

She knew her memory was not to blame after arranging everything back into the proper places. She sat down on the hygienist stool and said in a loud voice, "Okay, whoever you are, stop messing around! I want to get this job finished so that I can go home and watch a football game, so stop it! You have had your fun! Now let me go home!" It did not happen again while she was finishing up the job of cleaning the office. She went home and watched her football game quite pleased with herself. The next morning, I arrived at the office and began my ritual of checking the place out and turning on all the various switches in each room. When I turned on the lights in the hygiene room, I was greeted with a surprising pile of boxes of gloves, tissues, gauze, applicators, x-ray films, pens, and whatnot lying on the countertop. I assumed Penny had some sort of a problem the night before, but I could not guess what it might have been. I left the confusion for her to see rather than straighten it up before she arrived. When I showed her the room, she burst out laughing. "Well, whoever it was, he got the last word," she said. We decided Paco was the guilty party. We blamed him each time after that when something like this happened, and it did on many occasions.

On another occasion, I entered the hygiene room after turning on the lights and was greeted by the x-ray machine, pulled out into the room with the arm fully extended. These arms do not drift away from the wall on their own. It takes a bit of effort for that to happen, but there it was. It had to be Paco. At other times, the operating light would be placed in funny positions. One time it was turned upward toward the ceiling. Another time it was pulled away from the area much the way the x-ray machine had been pulled away from its normal resting position against the wall. Before replacing the disturbed objects to their correct positions, I would thank Paco for his little joke. I wondered at the time if he was laughing with me. I hope so.

I put the blame for another prank at Paco's feet that involved my mother. She was at the top of the stairwell on the south side, where Paco spent much of the time, about to turn and descend the stairs. Just ahead of her, a small piece of green paper caught her eye as it floated down into her line of sight. She told me that it changed course and began to drift down the stairs as if carried by an invisible hand held out flat with the paper resting in the palm. The paper crossed the landing and descended the lower flight of stairs. At that point, it fluttered to the floor as if the invisible hand had turned over and let it fall. Mom came to me, a bit shaken, and told me what she had seen. I was in the lab working on a case. I followed her to the top of the stairs where she pointed to the tiny green piece of paper lying on the carpet down at the foot of the stairs in the hallway below us. As she watched, I went down the stairs, picked up the paper, and returned to her with it. She held out her hand with the paper on her palm. "It was as if someone were carrying it like this," she said. I examined the paper. It was a torn ticket, like the ones handed out at a raffle. I had never seen a green one, however. My mother indicated that she had never seen it before and had no idea how it would have been drifting down from above her in such a way that she did not see it before she turned to take the first step. Where that ticket stub came from is a mystery that remains unsolved to this day. Paco? He has my vote.

We did not blame Paco for an odd event that Julia experienced on that same stairwell. As she was going down the stairs to meet a patient in the business office, she was stopped in her tracks by the sound of some animal growling. Not a dog, but the deep growl of a much larger animal. No one else had ever heard anything like that.

In the front room on the south side of the office, we have space for old files and record books for the various services we employ. There are ship models, antique pieces of furniture, and numerous paintings and photographs. One large armoire in a corner of the room seems to have some history attached to it of a paranormal nature. Many paranormal investigators I have had over the years have encountered a fussy older fellow who many have believed to have been a watch repairman. There's one clock in the room on a mantle that surrounds a fake fireplace (that I placed in the room just as a decorative piece); I bought it just because I liked it. The clockworks inside the thing are a real mess, but I bought the clock just for its appearance, not to tell time. In that room, with a grumpy old fellow who might have been a timepiece fix-it man, I have noticed that over the years the hands on the clock face have continued to move. It could be a mechanical oddity, but it is a rare case of a stopped clock working from time to time without a wound spring and frozen gears. Odd indeed.

Figure 9: The lunchroom window as viewed from the parking lot. The mysterious ghost of a woman with black hair would part the lower curtains and watch for someone unknown.

19

Curious Visitors Begin to Arrive

On March 13, 2010, Janet, our son Jason, and I were taking Janet's sister-in-law and her daughters on a tour of the office. Jason set his smart phone on record and placed it on the newel post of the railing of the stairs on the north side. We ended our tour at the top of the stairs. All the women began an impromptu session standing around the newel post with the phone still on top of it. After asking several questions and waiting a few seconds to allow time for an answer, they decided to end the session. Each in turn said good-bye and started down the stairs to leave the office. Once outside, Jason began listening to his recording, fast-forwarding, and stopping at random spots on the recording. Suddenly his eyes expressed surprise.

"Oh my gosh!" he said as he laughed, "listen to this!" As each of the women listened to the segment Jason kept setting his phone to, she also responded with surprise and some words similar to Jason's. Between the various ways of saying good-bye that the women had said in turn was the unmistakable voice of Lavina saying, "Bye, bye!"

Later that year, our niece, who lived at that time in Charleston, South Carolina, had told her story about the recorded "Bye, bye" on Jason's cell phone to her friends and coworkers. Five of them were inspired to come to the area and see the office for themselves. Shortly before lunch, Janet and I took the girls on a tour. Once concluded, they headed down the walk between the two buildings toward the parking lot in the back. I was locking the front door. As I made my way to the parking lot, I heard all the girls screaming, "Oh my god! Oh my god!" I darted down the remaining few feet of walkway to the corner of the building. There were all the girls in the lot beside their parked cars, facing the back of the building and looking up at the window where the snack room is located. Some were holding their hands to their mouths, some were jumping up and down, and some were pointing at the window. They had all seen the mysterious woman standing there with her hands parting the curtains. They saw her drop the curtains and back away. So, they got what they came for. They all saw a ghost, not on a dark rainy night in at graveyard, but on a pleasant spring day just before lunch, and looking through parted curtains right back at them.

One of the toys at the top of the stairs was a soft plastic ball. It was about the size of a child's bowling ball. From time to time, it was moved about in the hallway, but the furnace vent right at the top of the stairs could be the cause of that. Also, the floor in the upper hallway is slanted toward the stairs from settling, which the foundation workers were unable to correct. I decided to move the ball to the far end of the hallway away from the outlet and place it in a corner there where the slope of the floor would cause the ball to have to move uphill if it moved.

In April of 2010, the ball did something I did not expect. Although it did not leave the corner, it managed to rotate so that the area of the ball that looks like a belly button was no longer at the north pole of the ball, but down at equator level. No natural force I know of would do that, especially since the box of chocolates about ten feet away at the other end of the hallway was still intact. It is unlikely a mouse would turn down chocolates for a chance to play with a ball.

Penny was in operatory 1 on April 22, 2010, cleaning instruments. Through the x-ray window, she saw in operatory 2 a white fog-like thing about the size of a person but without any particular shape. At first she thought it was Becky entering the room through the back passageway into operatory 2, but when looking directly at it, she realized it was not. "It" meandered away from the window area, around the stools and the dental chair, and made its way toward the doorway into operatory 1 where Penny was standing at the counter. She said she fully expected to see it come into the room where she stood, but it did not. It just vanished

At the same time, Becky and Julie, the hygienist, were at the front desk discussing, of all things, the apparent increase in paranormal activity in the office. Becky told Julie that she, Julie, was the only one among the employees who had not seen a ghost. With that, Becky addressed the unseen "Others" to show themselves to Julie! Then she headed toward the storage room to retrieve a box of typing paper. While Becky was away from the

135

front desk, Julie felt a creepy cold sensation on her left arm. She said it was like refrigerated air. But when Becky returned with the box of paper, Julie decided not to tell her what seemed to be beside her. When Becky had settled in to her chair at the computer, she put her arms tightly around herself and said that suddenly she was freezing. This cold sensation lasted several minutes for both of them. It seemed to move from one to the other. Was it the same entity that had put its icy arms around Julia while she sat alone in the same area? Whatever it was, it left, and the air temperature in the workplace returned to normal for the rest of the day.

In May 2010, Janet and I had some friends visiting from Atlanta, Phil and Peg. The tour was of an artsy nature, involving the objects of art in the place rather than a tour having anything to do with ghosts. Peg is a wonderful watercolorist. She was interested in seeing the paintings and other art pieces in the office, and we had a lively discussion from the standpoint of one artist to another. As Phil and Peg were coming down the stairwell looking at the many paintings that now hang there, Peg suddenly noted the scent of a particular flower. She thought it odd that the flower she smelled would be in the office at that time. Room freshener? Perhaps? She asked me how I managed that scent in the stairwell.

I had no idea what she was talking about, since my nose has long been set on almost zero sensitivity to smells. Her husband began to pick up on it too by this time. Peg said it was really getting strong for her. Janet was beside me in the hallway and began to pick up on it, too.

"Lilac?" asked Janet.

"Viburnum, I would say," answered Peg. Janet agreed it might be viburnum. "They bloom earlier than this in Atlanta. Do they bloom in May around here?"

"I don't think so," answered Janet. Phil and I were unable to contribute much of value to this conversation. I told Peg that there was a female ghost who liked her and wanted to greet her with this floral scent. Peg was impressed and charmed by this unexpected gift. None of us felt the least frightened by it. It was a gift across time from one gracious lady to another. How could that be something to be afraid of?

Oddly enough, near the end of that month, I went up to the front room on the north side to get my car keys to run a quick errand, and as I entered the room, I was greeted by a very strong scent of honeysuckle (the one bloom I can pick up on and identify). I decided to try something. I walked to the opposite corner of the upstairs and returned to the room with the scent. It was still there, but to my poor inefficient nose, it was faint. I said, "Thank you," and left on my errand.

In July 2010, my sister, Ellen, and my brother-in-law, Bill, were in town from their home in St. Louis for his high school reunion. Their two sons are interested in paranormal subjects, and seeing an opportunity, they asked Bill to go through the office with a cassette recording machine and see if he could catch something on tape. Janet and I took Bill and Ellen down to the office after dark. Upon arrival, I sprinted ahead of everyone, turning on lights to set up our walk through the place. Bill turned on his recorder, and I had an EMF monitor with me to help in our little investigation. In the waiting room is a carousel horse from

137

Camden Park, an old local amusement park. Some time ago, the wooden Spillman Horses were removed and sold at auction. (Now, cast aluminum horses grace the carousel.) By this time, it was common knowledge that our little girl ghost spent a lot of time on that horse. I was telling Bill and Ellen this, and showing them the tarnished spot on the pole that supports the horse just where a child would place her hand while sitting on the horse. I turned on the monitor and discovered that it registered very high on the horse and on several chairs in the waiting room. "Someone is definitely here with us," I said. The monitor indicated that they were moving from the chairs toward the hallway. They passed Janet and Ellen on their way out of the room, and both reacted at the same time to a sudden cold sensation. They were very close at that moment to whomever left the room after getting up from the chairs.

For some reason, I thought that Lavina had gone up the stairwell too, so I said, "Let's go upstairs and see if we can contact the little girl up there."

"I'm right here!" she answered in a playful voice. Unfortunately, this was not heard by us but was on the tape. When we played the recording back, the quality of the sound was poor, but we heard Lavina answer that she was still right there on the horse. Bill was excited. He wanted to hear her again. He pushed the rewind button and stopped it. We stood there listening to total silence. Suddenly he realized that he was not on play but record. He frantically hit stop and rewind. This time he hit play. Unfortunately, he had successfully erased his only recording of a ghost caught on that night. His disappointment was palpable. Ellen was in that quietly steaming mood. A husband had once again made a mistake in the course of human history adding one more strike against husbands in general. But at least they had both heard her once.

Figure 10: The antique porcelain dolls. One turned on its side. The Barbie doll with one arm raised. The box of candy was left undisturbed.

20

The Special Message from Jim

Jim was a big man. He was a plumber. His booming voice could be heard all over the office. Surprisingly, he was well read. He read and wrote poetry, studied mathematics, physics, philosophy, history, and chemistry. We had many long discussions after his appointments at our office, which were always made at the end of the day. That way, he and I could talk long into the night after everyone else had left the office.

When he had appointments with Julie, he would fuss so loud you could hear him in every room complaining about the right-hand rest on her dental chair. It did not snap into place as it should when patients were seated for their hygiene appointments. He said over and over that some day he would come in with a bunch of tools, take the chair apart, and fix that hand rest once and for all.

Jim was one of the people who left toys for Lavina at the top of the stairs. His gift for her was two little porcelain dolls. Before we could see Jim, he first had to check on the dolls. We could hear him up there telling Little

Girl to move those dolls so that he would know that she liked them. This went on for two years. Jim was becoming frustrated. I told him he was so big he probably frightened her, and that a softer approach might help, but that was just not his way. Year in, year out, we heard, "Now, Little Girl, doggone-it, move these dolls!" As it turned out, he was about the size of the ghost we called Big Guy. The similarity might not have been lost on Lavina. The assistants just laughed.

On the fourth of July, 2010, Jim was sitting in a lawn chair on his patio. He was smoking a cigarette. He quietly died as he sat. The cigarette he was holding between his fingers had gone out as a result of the evening dew. That was on the weekend.

On Monday, Julie came into operatory 1 and asked if I would check on something for her. I left my patient, wondering what was wrong.

"Test the arm of my chair," she said. I moved it out of locked position and back into locked position. It had not done that for years. "Did you fix it?" she asked. "No...Do you suppose...?" I said.

"It was Jim. He always said he would fix that arm, some day," Julie said. Then I remembered one of our discussions that had involved the afterlife. He said that if he died first, he would give me a sign, and I told him that I would do the same if I went first. Now, Jim had done it.

A few weeks later, I noticed the little porcelain dolls. The doll on the right had been rotated ninety degrees to the left. It had been leaning at almost a forty-five-degree angle from the floor against a very narrow part of the turned spindle. Anything that would have struck the doll causing it to rotate from facing straight ahead from the spindle balustrade to a position where it was leaning on the same spot on the spindle, but on the right side of its head, would have caused the doll to roll off the spindle. The other doll beside it was not affected. A Barbie doll sitting on the floor further down along the banister had her left arm raised as if to say, "Hi!" The blue ball had been spun on a horizontal axis with the "belly button" transferred from north pole to equator. I am convinced that Jim came in, had a conversation with Lavina, and perhaps the two of them moved the toys. I like to think so. The hand rest in Julie's room still works.

Figure 11: The lunchroom window where a mysterious woman parts the curtains and looks out over the parking lot.

21

The Females Upstairs

One of my assistants, Sharon, had moved away for several years but was back in the area for a time. She needed some dental work and so, while treating her, we caught up on what had been going on in our lives. She related a story that I was never made aware of for whatever reason. She said that on one day, she had been eating her lunch alone in the office while the rest of us ran errands, as often happens. The time was close to one o'clock, and she made her way through the long room upstairs toward the hallway to go down to the front desk. As she passed through that room, she noticed something at the far end on the north side. It was a little girl leaning into the room from behind the doorway on that side. She had long dark hair beyond shoulder length, which was hanging down as she leaned straight out with only her head and neck showing. Sharon backed up to make sure of what she had seen, but the girl was not there. As far as I remember, that was the first time I had ever heard Sharon say anything about ghosts.

145

The mysterious woman in the snack room would appear now and then with no indication of who she was or why she looked out of that window. One of the paranormal teams was getting together with me in operatory 2. We were discussing the areas where the team might be most likely to pick up some data on their recording equipment. One member of the team arrived late. When she found us in the back of the building, she counted noses and asked another female team member who the woman was upstairs. I picked up on their chatter and joined in. It became clear that she had seen someone in the upstairs window holding back the curtains with her hands. When the woman in the window saw that someone was watching her, she quickly pulled back, letting the curtains drop. It was this action that caused the investigator to be curious. She may have thought that there was someone up there who should not be, or perhaps it was some sort of a joke. We got matters straightened out, however, and the team was informed that one member and her husband were one ghost ahead of the rest of the team, if they were keeping score.

December of that year brought me closer than I would ever knowingly be to the woman in the window. It was lunchtime. Julia, Julie, and Jill, the Three Js, were going to have their meal at one of the fast food emporiums in the area. I was going to have my lunch over some paperwork, so I stayed behind. I climbed the stairs on the south side and turned to my right to go down the hallway toward the snack room. To my utter surprise, there in front of the window was the mystery woman. She turned from the window, scooting one of the chairs at the table in the process, and

146

rushed away from my line of sight as I watched this baffling scene from the doorframe. As if running to catch a departing plane, she flew from the window with a total lack of decorum. Once out of my sight, the bustle and crash-bang clatter of her unceremonious egress came to an abrupt end. I arrived in the room looking to my right, but not expecting to see her, and turned to the chair that came very close to being tipped over. I sat down and said, "Look, you do not have to run and hide from us. Not one person here would ever harm you in any way, so please, do not be afraid of us."

My little speech did nothing. She may not have even been there to hear it, but at least I had tried to reach her. She was taller than I had thought. I would say about five feet, eight to ten inches. She had black hair, a blouse of some fashion that I could not place but was white, and a full skirt that was black. From the way she ran from me, I would say she was truly afraid. I do not know, of course, but I suspect it has something to do with rules. Perhaps she is simply not allowed to be seen for some reason. Who knows? She may be as afraid of living people as living people are afraid of ghosts.

22

Gifts and Threats

The most unusual and bizarre incident that happened to me involved my glasses. One of the lenses had popped out of the frame. I was upstairs in the front room on the north side. I tried to get the lens to pop back in, but I could not get it to go into place. I keep one of those glasses repair kits in operatory 1. I went down, found the kit, and returned to the room upstairs where my glasses and lens were lying on a table. To my utter and complete amazement, the lens was in the frame! I stood there squinting at the glasses. I picked them up from the table and turned them over and over in my hands. How? Jim, again? "Thanks, whoever you are. I really appreciate this!" I said out loud. How does one explain such things? I still have trouble believing it to this day, but it happened. That was January 2011.

Paco was busy in Julie's room again. He found that if he exchanged the instruments hanging in their holders, none of them would work. Several times Julie had this prank pulled on her. It had to be Paco. Surely.

In May, Jill was upstairs briefly near the snack room. She was about to return downstairs when she heard sounds like someone was setting out dishes in preparation for a meal. She wondered who it might be but did not check to see. She just assumed it was me, but upon arriving in operatory 2, she found me gloved, masked, and hard at work on a patient. She asked if I had been upstairs, in full knowledge that I could not have been. When I verified what she already knew, she realized she had heard a ghost. Was it the woman in the window? I think it was.

Morgan and I were in operatory 1. The patient had left, and we were cleaning the room. In the hallway above us, we heard the distinct sound of someone running back and forth from the front room to the back room and back again. Of our three dogs, Molly is one heavy-footed little gal. As Morgan and I listened, I assumed Janet had come into the office with Molly, and since it was lunchtime, Molly was turned loose to run upstairs. I mentioned to Morgan that I was sure Molly was up there, but I had heard that same sound before, and it always turned out to be Lavina. "Well, I hope it is Molly!" she replied. When we finished in the operatory, we went out to the front desk expecting to see Janet and Molly. Neither had been in the office. We told Becky, who was working the front desk, what we had heard. She had not heard the footfalls on her side of the building. Had it been Lavina after all? It was some little child, so Lavina was the. best guess.

About this same time, I was closing up the office at the end of the day. This involves flipping a great number of switches in a fairly good number of rooms. I was on the second floor, walking down the hallway above the hygiene room, when the voice of a man who would have had to have been well over six feet in height said above my right ear, "*Get outta here!*" The voice had a deep growl to it. It was loud and clear. It sounded as if it came from a live person. It was so real I jumped to my left and whirled around at the same time, expecting to see a very large man standing there. The hallway was dark and empty. "Get out of here yourself!" I answered. I stood there looking around. I was certain I would see something, but there was nothing visible, no static electricity, and no more sound.

I kept looking around as I descended the stairwell. Whatever it was seemed to have left the area. Had it been watching as I made my rounds through the room turning off lights and equipment? Was this the start of a new set of events in which subtle encounters would transform into unsettling words spoken directly to me and my staff? The thing we called Big Guy seemed to be the one doing the frightening things. The other entities gave little signs that were more like practical jokes. So Big Guy was. probably changing his tactics in order to get our undivided attention, or was he actually wanting the place to himself? Did Mrs. Bowen have problems with this aggressive thing, causing her to sell the home she had lived in for almost two decades?

These questions were spinning around in my head as I locked the front door and walked to the parking lot in the rear of the office.

23

Leota

A medium named Leota, who lives in Florida, heard about the hauntings and contacted me to set a date to visit the place. Her husband, Tim, came with her. The two worked very well together, with him as the skeptic and her as the believer. When they arrived at the office, he got as far as the waiting room and found so many artifacts that he was interested in, he stopped to look at them. Tim, Janet, and I engaged in a lively conversation about the items on display there. Meanwhile, his wife was drawn up the stairwell to the room above the waiting room. She was led there by a little girl named "Livy" as she told us afterward. She assumed the girl's name was Olivia, thinking that "Livy" was a nickname for Olivia. Later, I asked Leota if the child's name might be Lavina. She had never heard of that name but said it did make more sense for "Livy" to be a nickname for Lavina.

Livy took her to the window at the front of the building overlooking Twentieth Street. She told Leota that her bed was across the windows, with the one side of the

151

bed against the windows. The medium did not know at the time that Livy had a mother and sister who slept in the room with her. (I had asked Leota if she wanted a history of the events that we had experienced in the place, but she had refused, stating that would make it difficult for her to get a clear reading of the place.) The little girl also had a Victorian-style chair at the foot of the bed, which she enjoyed sitting in. She also showed Leota the closet in the corner where she and another little girl played—and hid from Big Guy when things became difficult. This closet was soon afterward known as Livy's closet. We three had joined Leota in the front room. At this point in the session, the medium sensed the presence of a male in the room with us. He was checking us out and was satisfied we meant no harm and left. "He is a protector for Livy," she said. He had circled me several times as I stood there according to Leota. We are not sure, but the other girl Livy called Sara may have been her sister using an alias. We already knew that Livy used aliases, and this other child could just as easily have used them too. Young girls can be deceptive, so the information the medium received from them could have been made up.

One detail Leota learned from them was that they enjoyed sitting on the bed at the front window and looking out the window at the traffic on Twentieth Street. Livy also showed her the blue blanket on her bed. She seemed to indicate that the blue blanket was special to her. Leota sat on the floor and talked to the girls. Her hair is very long, and when she said that one girl was playing with her hair in the back, I slowly stepped around her to see if I could see any evidence of that. Sure enough, strands of her hair were being pulled away, and they were falling back as if let go. There was no doubt in my mind that this was a genuine contact and not some form of deception. The strands pulled away and fell back every few seconds. I have seen children who are fascinated with an adult's hair, pull strands away, and let it fall back just like those strands of the medium's hair. The girls seemed to be interested in her long hair. "Braids. Sara has braids," Livy said, according to Leota.

Suddenly Leota said she felt a choking, burning sensation in her throat. Thinking that one of the girls was trying to communicate the story of the house in Ohio that burned, I quickly related the gist of the fire story, but she said the choking sensation was not smoke related. It was something else. She could not understand what the burning in her throat meant, but she said that to the girls it was important. We were left with more unanswered questions. Leota assured us that at some point it would be made clear to us what the burning throat meant.

Seeing the girls go into and out of the closet, the medium suggested that I move the toys to the closet from the hallway at the top of the stairwell. This way, when frightened by something, they could have their toys in there with them. The toys were quickly transferred to the closet. The girls also told her they wanted chocolate candy in there with the toys, so Janet took some chocolate from the business office area and put the pieces on the floor with the toys. The girls tried to close the closet door. It quivered for about thirty seconds before we figured out what they wanted. They finally asked the medium for help, and she closed the door. She told us that they wanted to be left alone in there, so we left the room, went down the hall and into the long room.

The medium stopped, looking at the wall at the far end. She looked confused. She said that she thought there was a window on that wall. I reminded her that she had come up the stairs while we were in the waiting room discussing the objects on display. She had turned on no lights; she did not know where the light switches were located, and Livy had hurried her upstairs as well, so her first view of the upstairs was made in the dark. She first saw Livy in an oval-backed Victorian chair in a darkened room. She had then entered the dark long room and saw a woman standing in the room who seemed to be French, from what Leota could make of her speech. She saw at the far end of the dark room a double window with drapes and sheers.

In the light, both rooms looked totally dissimilar to what she had seen in the dark. The Victorian chair with dark-red velvet upholstery became a black-simulated leather and chrome Danish modern design. The wall with the double window became a solid wall with a mural. I could see where her confusion would come in.

The woman she saw in the long room she described as having medium brown hair tied neatly up in a Gibson Girl style. Her light-colored dress was full length and of Edwardian design. She was young with a full round face. Several paranormal investigators had made recordings of a woman who spoke in a foreign language that they could not identify. I heard them myself and could not make out the language either. The recordings were so full of static it would be hard to understand her if she spoke English, but French was one of the likely languages.

We were walking along the length of the long room, and the medium stopped at the saddle that rested on a wooden base covered with a gray blanket. At one time, the saddle had been in the middle of the waiting room. It was placed there for children to play on and sit on. As with most of my ideas concerning my young patients, they usually ignored the saddle. The adults, on the other hand, loved to sit on it. As more children's specialists came into the area, the number of children I treated had been reduced to about a dozen. I decided to remove the saddle because it had become more of a hazard than an asset. I felt one of my older patients might somehow stumble over it. I moved it to the long room, and that was where the medium found it. As she bent over the saddle and placed her hands on it, she said Livy rushed up to it and put her hands on it, too. "This is special," she said. "It means a lot to Livy." I knew Livy liked the saddle. My electromagnetic field monitor had found her on it many times, as had many paranormal investigators. Livy liked horses.

As we continued to the end of the room and turned right to enter the snack room, the medium mentioned that at the window that faces the parking lot there is a woman who watches for someone to come to her. She said the woman was not there just then, but she left some sort of energy that the medium could faintly read. I told her of all the people who had seen her, including the screaming bevy of girls from Charleston, South Carolina.

As Leota's husband and I wandered down the hallway toward the south-side stairwell, Janet and the medium wandered into the back room on the north side. They were talking about a piece of needlework that we have that is very old and French. At that moment, the French woman the medium had seen in the adjacent room on her impromptu excursion to the second floor came into the room while Janet was describing the French needlepoint artifact. The ghost apparently stays in this area of the building. Perhaps during her lifetime, she had rented those two rooms. Another possible reason for her presence is a portrait I purchased. It is of a woman wearing a scarf. She has a sad expression. The French ghost may be somehow tied to that painting.

For whatever reason, the ghost began speaking in French with great animation. Leota suspected the lady was excited about what Janet had said, but there was no way to be sure. Janet called to me to join them, so we two husbands did as told, and entered the small room where our wives were talking. Leota's husband spoke a little French and upon her prompting, began asking our invisible guest questions in broken French. His stumbling grammar made the spirit laugh and clap her hands. She would not give her name but said in English that she was twenty-nine. We decided we would walk into the snack room as Tim asked her more questions. She stopped at the wall that divided the building into the two halves, so she was not the mystery woman in the snack room window.

We ambled through the long room's south end and down the hall to the front room on that side. This is the room with the fake fireplace and the stopped clock on the mantle. In the far corner is an antique English armoire. This caught Leota's attention. She saw a little old man who might be a locksmith or watch repairman. He had a great number of very small instruments lying about. He did not wish to communicate with Leota at all. He just wanted to work at his workplace. He may have been the one who fiddled with my very dead mantle clock. He would not discuss anything with Leota, in spite of her repeated attempts to befriend him. He just wanted to be left alone so that he could get on with his work. We left him there.

We walked around the entire upstairs one last time before returning to the north stairwell. As we passed the two upstairs restrooms, the medium sensed something that was not good in both of them. She did not indicate what was there at all. She did not want to enter either of them. She then sat down on the steps on the north side. We discussed the portrait of Livy there on the wall. She was older in the painting, and her face was much thinner than that of the girl Leota saw, but she said it was without a doubt the same girl.

Leota settled herself on the second step of the stairwell next to the front bedroom door, intending to see if the little girl would come out of the room and tell her anything more. We left her alone on the stairs to try some "girl talk" with Livy. Apparently, Livy did emerge; this was when the medium discovered she enjoyed sunshine while sitting on her bed at the front window. This pleasant interlude was interrupted by the sound of scratching on the wall at the landing below. This was followed by loud and distinct sounds of footfalls behind them coming from the long room into the hallway in front of Livy's room. Assuming the noise was us returning to the stairwell, Leota looked up, but no one was there. She had been singing

"Frere Jacques" to Livy, but when the medium turned back toward the girl, Livy had vanished again. Surprised, Leota looked over her shoulder again to see what could be making the sound.

It was then that she felt the vibration on the wooden step behind her—as though someone very heavy had just stepped onto the staircase. With the next thump of a heavy foot, the step on which Leota was sitting shuddered and gave slightly under an unseen weight. The footsteps proceeded down the stairs, resonating in the stairwell, and Leota followed the sound with her eyes as a thump deliberately came from each individual step, hard enough to feel the vibrations from her seat at the top. The thumping crossed the landing and continued down the lower set of stairs in the same manner, and then suddenly stopped. Once she realized what had just happened, the medium knew this was one ghost she should avoid. She continued singing the "Frere Jacques" tune but changed the words of the song to "Bill and Janet, please come here!" But we did not hear her. Her husband came to the rescue, unwittingly, by coming up the same set of stairs. He had not heard Big Guy. They discussed the experience she had with the ghost of a big man. Tim was certain that she had been hearing *him* as we were descending the opposite stairwell on the south side. He asserted Leota was hearing our footfalls through the wall that separated the two stairwells.

When Janet and I arrived on the spot where Tim and Leota were discussing the sounds that had frightened her, we decided to test Tim's theory that she had heard him on the north side and us on the south side. I went back to the south-side stairs and literally stomped as I ascended and descended the stairs several times. Tim also retraced his steps several times. When we returned to where the ladies were sitting on the stairs, we were told by both of them that they could barely hear us. We had not made the sounds she had heard. I told them that when I bought the place the north stairs had never been carpeted. There were no holes from carpet tacks anywhere on those stairs. Leota then realized the sound was of a heavy man on bare floors and stairs.

I proceeded to relate to Leota the information I had about the one we called Big Guy. She was certain we were describing the same entity. I then told her about one paranormal group whose research had uncovered a newspaper article about a man they suspected was Big Guy who had hanged himself in my building. Unfortunately, I never saw the article, and the group could not find it in their research materials. They assumed it had been accidentally deleted. They told me what they could remember of the article they had found in the Cabell County Library. The individual's name was John. They could not remember his last name. Leota and I decided we would call Big Guy John from that time onward. We were talking about this possibility. That was when "John" came on the scene. Leota saw him. She said he was wearing a rumpled brown suit without a tie and a dirty grayish shirt. He wore a farmers' type of brogan high-top shoes. He staggered about and had a shuffling, stumbling, drunkard's way of walking. He was angry. He insisted that his name was not John, and that he did not hang himself there in the building or anywhere else. Leota said he was a blustering, bullying, arrogant drunk. He was furious with us, seeming to be more sensitive about his reputation than his appearance. He said over and over, "Listen to me. You don't understand!" Except for pushing Leota several times, he was not physically abusive to us. His behavior seemed more bent toward correcting my mistaken account of suicide on his part than with trying to bully us with his ghostly physical strength. He kept saying that "Will was wrong."

Leota did not tell me that while all this was going on. It was not until several days later that she said Big Guy had told her that I was wrong. As it turned out, he was telling the truth. A man did hang himself, but it was at 1125 Nineteenth Street, one block west of my building. We did also come to the conclusion that our John was not the one who killed himself. This clumsy oaf was just a drunk who had a very high opinion of himself and was the one who stomped around and slammed doors. Thanks to Leota, I had a mental image that I could put with the sounds I had heard so many times in the office over forty years, but I still did not know who he was.

Janet asked Leota if she had encountered Paco. Janet liked Paco. He was her kind of ghost. A bit of a clown, not one to fear. The medium drew a blank. She said there was no Paco she had seen. She said that was too bad because her Spanish was a lot better than her French. I noted that we really had not spent much time at all in his area. That is why he probably did not reveal himself to her. While standing with us in the waiting room, she said in Spanish using a loud voice, "Sorry, Paco, I didn't know! See you next time!" With that, she saw in the doorway leading to the hallway on the other side a tiny head with black hair pop out from behind the door facing, and with a big grin said, "Si!" That was it for Paco. He was like that—pop in, pop out.

As she left the office with us, the medium remembered one thing that she had not told us. The number 1809. To someone in the office, it was important. Was it a date or something else? I never found out.

Upon reflection, this session impressed me greatly. The medium went into the office without being told anything about it. She went right to areas that had the majority of the spiritual connections. She made her way through the place unerringly right to the closet where the girls hid, the saddle where I and a host of researchers had spotted Lavina, and she gravitated to the correct side of the building without hesitation. Later she told us that Livy had led her through much of that excursion. She found that Lavina preferred to be called Livy. This seems so natural for a girl to shorten Lavina to Livy. All of us had seen the closet door quiver as if someone was trying to close it. Finally, she could not make strands of her long hair pull away from her head and fall back repeatedly as I watched. Her seeming familiarity with the place and her knowledge of people we ourselves could not see or hear provided me with information that would be made clear later in my dealings with those who worked very hard to uncover what had happened in that place. I believe the session was genuine. I believe the medium was being honest. She received nothing for her findings. In fact, she came to the office at her own expense. As a result of these observations and her immediate reporting to us most of what she experienced as it happened, I am convinced that the session was not a prank. It was as it was presented to us—a person with a gift, sharing that gift with us as a favor, and nothing else. It was beautiful.

Figure 12: The north end of a long room. The bookcase to the left was formerly a doorway into the back room. From the bookcase, a black mist was seen crossing in front of the suit of armor and entering the hallway toward the stairwell.

24

Paranormal Investigations

Our new office cleaning lady, Stacy, began to experience odd occurrences as she worked in nearly every room in the office. On one occasion, she and her helper heard loud knocking over the clamor of two vacuum cleaners. Both women tried to find the source of the knocking but could not. Later, they saw figures here and there in the rooms that they would mistake for each other until they realized that the partner was nowhere nearby.

The sighting of full-bodied figures in the office by 2011 had become fairly common—almost as common as sounds that had no source we could explain. My assistant, Jill, was walking through the hallway leading to operatory 1 and saw what she thought was me on the stairs. She later said that she thought that I was walking up the stairway. But as she entered operatory 1, she saw me at the counter washing my hands in the sink. She immediately backed up and looked into the stairwell and seeing that no one was there, told me what she had just observed. She said she thought it was me because he had green on, like a green suit. I asked her if it could have been a brown suit. She thought about it for a minute and conceded that it might have been brown. She said she expected it to be me, so she just assumed whoever it was had on green scrubs. When she realized it might have been brown, she asked me how I knew the person was wearing brown. I answered that I had come to believe that Big Guy might wear a brown suit. She found that unsettling.

On October 15, 2011, Lawrence County Ghost Hunters were set up in the office to conduct an investigation. One of the female team members was sitting in a chair on the north-side front room. She had brought the blue ball from the hallway into the room where she sat. She watched as the ball rolled across the floor from the door to the opposite corner where the closet door is located. She also experienced spells of chills in the room and reported having a conversation with two little girls in the room using a ghost box. This relatively new instrument is supposed to pick up and play the voices it gathers by spanning radio frequencies in rapid cycles. The voices of the ghosts that are speaking nearby are transmitted as computer-generated sounds that the machine forms into words. Often, these electronic voices come up with words that are hard to accept as statements made by spirits. They seem more like random words that have no meaning. The random words are interpreted by the investigators as they see fit.

I prefer recordings of the actual ghost voices rather than the mechanical-sounding words the ghost box makes. I always thrill to the sound of Livy's voice as she speaks into a recorder. This team, however, preferred the ghost box with its robot-sounding "voice." A lot of the teams have gone to this type of technology. I hate it. For me, it represents a step backward in the efforts to learn about these fascinating phenomena.

One of the other team members was in the hygiene room with a recorder. He got Paco to say his name, and you could hear him say it with his Mexican accent. That has so much more evidential value than a robot voice that has no gender, inflection, or accent revealed. All that information is lost using those machines. Many investigators also use a K-2 meter. This detects the movement of a ghost as opposed to air currents, or even people. Often investigators were able to get Paco and Livy to cause the K-2 meters to light up when asked. All these and other machines were used by the teams and only rarely did they fail to produce evidence of intelligent haunting. Intelligent hauntings are those that demonstrate responses to requests either vocally or by action. Either way, the spirit is recorded as it interacts with the investigator. I have heard Livy's charming voice on so many recordings that I can easily recognize her.

A local radio station contacted the office and set up a date and time to broadcast from the office. The date they wanted to have their program air was October 31, 2011. They would have their early-morning personalities do their regularly scheduled program after having spent the night in the office. Cliff and Jill arrived with a technician in the early hours of the thirty-first as we had agreed. Along with this trio were several other people who were just interested in witnessing what would happen during the night. I brought an air mattress to the office and set it up in the long room at the north end. As it turned out, Cliff had his own air mattress, and he set his up in the same room, but on the south end. Jill elected to use the air mattress I had provided. She said she would use it to take breaks during the night from time to time.

For the pair, it would be an opportunity to set up a few jokes and gags. There was never any notion of having a serious scientific investigation. I understood this and fully expected a lighthearted approach would be the mind-set for their stay. I was surprised to see that they did not bring any equipment at all with them to record sounds that they could play back during their radio broadcast. The lack of any effort to set up a format that could really start public interest in the show told me that not a lot of thought had been put into their planning. I decided I would soldier on and be a good host. There was no time to try to change the direction things were taking.

Then something interesting occurred. Cliff left the office, for some reason, leaving Jill with me. As we broke the ice with small talk, I began to pick up on the fact that she might actually be interested in learning about just what a paranormal investigation consists of. I jumped into a crash course on the subject. I ran up to the front room on the second floor and brought down two EMF meters. I explained to Jill the basic concept behind the function of the meters and how they were found to be able to pick up the energy that ghosts seem to consist of. I turned on one of the meters, gave it to Jill, and explained what would happen if a ghost came nearby, having her hold it near an electrical outlet. The electromagnetic field around the outlet caused the meter to measure the strength and location of

166

the field. Then I explained that for reasons not completely understood, the meter would do the same thing if a ghost came close to it.

As Jill sat in one of the waiting room chairs holding the meter, it began to record a field that was getting closer to her as it slowly responded with ever-increasing beeps and a higher level on the analog gauge. "What is this doing?" she asked. "You are in the presence of a ghost," I answered. At that point, one of the people present told me he wanted to take some pictures of her holding the meter since that might be the only evidence anyone would gather the whole night. "Please do!" I replied. He began to take pictures as the meter recorded stronger and stronger responses to the field near Jill. Another person in the room took the other meter and held it out in front of Jill.

"Look, this one is registering something too," he said. Then, at about that moment, both EMF monitors began to ramp down until they stopped registering any field in the area.

"Let's see if I got anything," said the fellow with the smartphone camera. He touched the phone with his thumb several times and on the screen appeared a series of photos. "Oh my god! Look at this!"

We all gathered around him. Across several of the photos were a series of fogged images. The fog came into the first photo on the left, and through the series of shots, it passed across the area in front of Jill. When the young man put the other EMF monitor near, his arm was visible in the shots taken at that point. His arm was in front of the fogged image. His arm was not fogged, but the image behind his arm was fogged. The series was taken in a fully

167

lit room with five people present. None of us saw the fog. None of us experienced anything that indicated what was passing by in front of Jill. I asked the young man if he would e-mail three of the shots that show the fog entering the frame from the left, centered in the next frame, and leaving the last frame on the right with the arm of the fellow holding the other meter.

These three pictures when presented in context of the circumstance in which they were taken offer very strong evidence of spiritual activity in that room, full of people, at the time. The two meters and the smartphone all acted at the same time as they responded to the electromagnetic field, or whatever it was, as the field passed between us. The fact that the arm was not fogged in the same frames in which the background was fogged eliminates the possibility of a malfunction in the smartphone, because the entire image including the arm would have been fogged if that had been the case. Lastly, the photographer showed us the shots immediately after taking them... He e-mailed the three shots that I chose as I watched. There was no manipulation of the pictures at any time. I am not sure Jill understood the value of the incident from the standpoint of the convergence of the phenomenon and the three machines with all of them starting, peaking, and falling off at exactly the same time.

Later that night, Jill had an interesting pair of events occur as she took breaks on the air mattress in the long room upstairs. She told me that she was lying on her back with her cell phone held up in front of her face. She was texting a friend. Above her head, a "dark thing, like a big puff of black smoke," came out from the bookcase behind her head and floated directly over her toward the doorway that opens into the hall. She texted her friend a brief description of what she had just seen. She thought it was a shadow caused by car headlights somehow and didn't think much about it. Later that night, as she was taking another break, the same thing happened again. She still did not consider it as a paranormal event, but only some sort of shadow cast in the room by headlights. She did not investigate the rooms to see if she could discern the reason for the very odd shadow, even though she had the lights on in all the rooms at the time.

Jill had another experience that night that she was certain was paranormal. In the upper room where Livy had died, Jill heard the sound of a child crying. That one event led her to think that there might be something to the stories told by people who had spent a night there.

The morning found Cliff, Jill, and the sound technician tired and rather disinterested in their time spent in the office in spite of a list of experiences that should have made them glad to have taken the time to stay there. Jill offhandedly told me about the whimpering sounds of a child in the bedroom where the girl had died. If I had heard whimpering sounds in a room where I knew a child had died, I would have marked it as a major paranormal experience. The black thing that drifted above her three times during the night in a fully lighted room failed to excite her. I explained the theory investigators had developed as a possible explanation for their occurrence. Such things are called residual hauntings. They are some form of energy of an unknown nature that replays events over and over. These things do not interact with anyone at any time. I showed her the video recording I had of the residual that had been caught on camera. She told me it looked just like what she saw, and it moved at the same speed as the three she saw passing over her. "You saw a ghost," I said as matter-of-factly as that. I am uncertain if I impressed her with that or not. I do think I got her thinking. It was a first step for her, but I have often wondered if that first step was also the last.

I think the residual haunting that I and several paranormal investigators have seen at the north end of the long room represents either Livy's mother or her sister running to the stairwell after Livy cried out from the landing. That would have been the start of a weeklong nightmare for the three women until, in death, Livy's suffering ended. That terrible moment would have been intense enough to cause the formation of a residual haunting. Jill was the first person I know of who saw the black residual in a fully lighted room. I know of none who saw it in daylight.

The technician told me about an interesting puzzle he could not solve. Before night was very far advanced, I had helped him set up a card table that I keep in the office and some folding chairs. On the table, he placed a laptop computer, the earphones for Jill and Cliff to use, and a microphone system that was connected to an extension arm. The extension arm was clamped to the card table. Early in the morning, the technician entered the waiting room to get the equipment ready to broadcast the show. The microphone and its arm had been removed from the table and placed in a corner of the room. No one admitted to doing that. Everyone seemed to be genuinely surprised.

Cliff told me that the only thing he had personally experienced was the cold air he felt on his neck when he reached the top of the stairs on the north side. He did investigate the air currents in the area and noted that there were no forced air outlets in the ceiling anywhere on the second floor. They were all mounted in the floors of every room. There were no cold air returns in any ceiling on the second floor either. He said the icy cold breeze he felt on the back of his neck would have to be counted as unknown. Unknown? Hardly. Not to me at least. For a small group of people with absolutely no knowledge of paranormal investigation, no equipment, no understanding of events that they did experience, and more interested in gags, giggles, and gaffs, I would say they had a very fruitful night.

It was time for the early-morning show. A guest was invited to help liven things up. She was one of the members of Huntington Paranormal Investigations and Research. This team did more research into the history of my office and the people who occupied it than any of the other paranormal groups. The young woman was asked a series of questions, and she responded well. I had to leave them to their banter as patients began to arrive. We escorted them past the impromptu radio station, the program was soon wrapped up, and our patients had something to talk about when they left the office. In retrospect, I think it was a good experience for everyone.

I think Jill would have a good deal of success as a ghost hunter. Some people have a talent for this activity, but only a few of those ever realize that talent because of the extremely unusual circumstances required before one

171

could even suspect he or she possesses it. Cliff, on the other hand, is a good example of the majority of humanity—no talent for attracting spirits. One could say that the ability to interact with the other side is a gift. As with the gift of artistic talent, being able to attract, interact, and perceive spirits improves through practice. One can practice every day with a musical instrument but practicing communication with ghosts is something most people would shrink away from, so there has to be something present beyond the talent. Additional factors must come into play. I feel that is why this talent becomes put up on a shelf in the back of one's mind and never exercised.

25

We Don't Believe in Ghosts...And Yet...

On October 4, 2011, my assistant, Jill, passed through the north-side stairwell on her way to operatory 1and thought she saw me going up the stairs. I was in a small room located within operatory 1 that was formerly our dark room for developing x-rays. We use it now as a closet. I heard footfalls on the stairs, and assumed Jill was going up the stairs. When she entered the operatory, she was shocked to see me in the dark room. I was equally surprised to see her in operatory 1 with me. We both asked the question, "Who was on the stairs?" Since I did not see anyone from where I was situated, I asked her if she saw anyone on the stairs. She said she thought she saw me.

On November 23, 2011, Jill saw a man on the stairs again, and again, she thought she saw me. She said the man had a greenish suit on. That was all she noticed. She was certain it was me in my dark-green scrubs. I asked her if the man might have been wearing a brown suit. Upon reflection, she said it was indeed brown, not green. She said she was so sure she was seeing me, the clothing was seen as green in order to put me on the stairs. We concluded she probably saw Big Guy. It took her a great deal of thought to believe in this idea. Because of her very strict church-oriented lifestyle, it was hard for her to accept, and I have to respect her for that.

I find that problem to be the case quite often in this area. Those people who have strong associations with their churches do not accept the concept of a spirit haunting a place. They can readily accept the notion that devils and demons infest a place, but not the spirits of normal people who have died. The teachings of the church run deeply into this subject and serious followers are dissuaded from even thinking about ghosts as real things in this universe. I do not try to upset that apple cart with counterarguments. It is pointless and harmful. When this point of view is expressed, I think the best answer is to agree to disagree, and let it go at that.

One patient saw something that had all of us scratching our heads. She was sitting in the dental chair in operatory 3, the hygiene room. The hygienist had left the room momentarily. While she was out at the business desk looking up a six-month appointment for the patient, Sydney saw a light under a closet door in the room. The door was located in front of her as she sat in the chair.

She did not know that the door led to a closet as she was watching the light going back and forth between the lower edge of the door and the floor; she assumed someone was on the other side looking for some small item with a flashlight. When Julie returned to her operatory, Sydney asked, "Where does that door lead to?" Julie opened the door to show Sydney that there was a closet, and that was all. The closet was originally a pantry and was never supplied with a light. Sydney proceeded to describe what she saw while Julie was out of the room. The two talked about the light and were still on the subject when I joined them for the examination part of the appointment. We all came to the conclusion that Sydney had witnessed a very unusual paranormal incident. It turned out to be unique in its character among all the incidences of unexplained sightings.

Sydney was thrilled to have been able to see something like that. She said it was just enough to satisfy her need to know for certain that odd things do indeed happen at the office but not scary enough to cause her to be upset. One could say she just wanted to sample the subject without diving in over her head. She was one of many patients who was willing to write in their own handwriting what was experienced and sign the entry. Many others backed away from the offer to write in our log what they had seen. Now that I think of it, none of those people who did write were frightened by what happened in their presence. They were just curious and rather matter of fact about it. Those who would not make entries in the book were upset in some way, to varying degrees. Perhaps those people were not able to resolve in their minds the conflict between their preconceptions about ghosts and the simple fact that they experienced events that challenged those preconceptions. Religion and the constraints it places on thinking in these areas would constitute a stumbling block for many.

Sydney is an example of a person who was taught by the church that ghosts are not real because the subjects of life and the afterlife are well covered in religious teachings. These teachings were accepted by her as the truth and nothing but the truth. Then along comes this office with its oddities that, for her, presented a conundrum. Who is right—the church or me and my strange office? Something had to give. As she was mulling this over in her head, an idea came to her. She decided to write a mystery novel about the ghost of a young girl who helps another young woman solve a murder mystery. This she did. And for Sydney, the idea of ghosts existing and those of her religious teachings would just have to get along somehow. Sydney had accepted the idea of the reality of ghosts without actually seeing or hearing anything. It was the stories about the hauntings at the office that tipped the scales for her. Then she saw something that verified the truth. I think she represents the type of person we all would do well to emulate; not just on the conflict between religious teaching and the existence of ghosts, but on any subject which, in the presence of evidence that conflicts with previously held dogma, the truth of the matter stands alone and wins the argument. That is something so many people are not able to do, but it is the key to the personality that frames a leader.

Another strange happening occurred on March 28, 2012. We were about to start a procedure when our patient, Jerry, suddenly jumped from a reclining to a sitting position. To accomplish that maneuver, he had activated nearly every muscle in his body. I was caught off guard and quickly backed away. At first, I thought the patient had some sort of medical problem that might be very serious. Jerry looked first at my assistant, Morgan, and then to me.

He looked around the room and then returned to his original recumbent position.

"Are you okay?" I asked as I assessed his vital signs. "Oh, I'm okay, but who was down there near my feet?" he asked.

"No one," I responded as I glanced at Morgan and then looked at him. Jerry told us, after he settled down a bit, that he had put his checkbook in his sock because he didn't want to be bothered with it, and he did not want to put it in his pants pocket. As we were preparing our instruments to start working, he felt someone pull his checkbook from his sock. He said it was over half way out by the time he jumped. After a discussion and some attempts to make the checkbook come up out of his sock, we decided a ghost was having some fun with him. We thought perhaps Paco might be the one who played the prank. If it was not Paco, he had a copycat prankster ghost with the gift of originality.

26

Hollywood Comes to Huntington

June 8, 2012, stands alone in this story as the most important event to unlock the mystery of what Livy wanted us to know…that for years she tried to communicate to me, and many others—who Big Guy actually was. Leota had broken ground when she got Livy to open up. Through her communication with Livy, we learned so many details about her and her world. We learned what Big Guy looked like in general. Through Leota, we filled in so many blanks; however, Big Guy was still an unknown in many ways. Leota was unable to see his face clearly, and he would not divulge his name, or anything of his personal life story to her. He only expressed anger at me for marking him as a suicide. From this agitated display, we concluded he had a very high opinion of himself and would go to great lengths to protect his memory as that of a good person who would never stoop to suicide—a drunkard who was worried about his reputation. One might throw into his personality profile that he was not able to think with any semblance of logic.

As the days unfolded from June 8, 2012, the story of Lavina Wall opened up to its full magnitude. All the dark corners were swept away, and everyone would learn what happened on the stairwell in October of 1929. The conflict between Lavina and Big Guy was about to be brought to light.

The details of the hauntings in the office were discussed with the producer of a television program that deals with paranormal investigations. The two key questions he needed the answers to were whether the story was genuine or not and if I would allow a film crew into my office to film a show that would be put on the air. I had no problem with the first question, and my frank answers convinced the producer that there was indeed a haunting taking place. The second question gave me reason to pause. I had to think about that. It is so often the case that film producers come to our area with flowery overtures and propositions dripping with kindness, only to twist their storyline into derisive slander. We become the butts of their jokes and jibes, and there is nothing that can ever be done by us to correct the damage. My greatest concern had to do with that possibility with their program. My wife and I had often watched the show, and they were always respectful of the people they came into contact with during the course of each story, but this would be a show about a haunting in West Virginia. How would we be portrayed? How would my staff and I be portrayed? There was a real risk involved. Should I open Pandora's box or not? At length, I signed on with the show and allowed them to tape a program in my office. I was a bit afraid. As it turned out, our area was not abused by the show in its final cut as it aired. To my relief, we were not treated with disrespect. For that, I thank the people involved in making the program.

There were several producers for the company who apparently had certain areas of oversight responsibility divided among them. The first producer actually was here at work one week before the others arrived. One task he was assigned was to take photos of every room in the office. I allowed him in after hours, and he quietly went through every room to take the pictures. I waited in the waiting room for him. I didn't want to bother him while he was working. When he came into the room where I was, we sat and talked for a time about what was about to take place. He was concerned with all the antique articles and paintings in my office. He explained that none of these articles could be in the rooms during filming. He asked me if I could arrange to have them removed. I looked around. In the waiting room alone were a considerable number of items. The task to somehow remove everything would be daunting.

"Frankly, I don't know how I can do that," I said.

"I don't either," he answered. "I'll tell you what. Just take away as much as you can to a safe place, and we will somehow take care of the rest. What can't be changed, we will cover up and shoot around."

That was something I had not considered. "I will see what I can do," I answered. We shook hands, and soon he was on a plane back to Hollywood.

When he arrived back on the job in California, he decided to look at the shots of the rooms he took while on his visit. He called me with a slight tremor in his voice. The four photos taken in the back room on the north side were all fogged. None of them could be used. He kept saying that he had a really good camera, and he could not understand how those four shots could have been fogged. "Do you suppose a ghost did that?" he asked. I told him about the photos that were fogged when the radio show personalities visited the office. He was quite taken aback by that. I think it shook him a little-well, more than a little.

Two weeks later, after many calls, e-mails, signed contracts, and hours spent taking away as much as I thought needed to be hidden, I hoped I was ready. I enlisted the help of a very good friend, Jeremy, who graciously agreed to give up his evening to help me with the work. We spent five hours removing and hiding everything that seemed to fit the instructions I was given by the producers and director. I was wrong.

I returned to the office after closing for the day to unlock it and greet the film crew. I was amazed at how many there were. They were all young and full of energy and fully focused on their jobs. They were to the last one a very impressive group of people. The first task they set upon was to remove and cover many of the objects Jeremy and I had left. They also had to tape over any names of the various pieces of dental equipment that might be visible in any of the shots that would be taken in the operatories. The crew labored from 5:00 to 10:00 PM, clearing and setting up drape material that in many rooms would cover entire walls, ceiling to floor. While this was taking place, the crew experienced some paranormal activity of their own. Scissors, nails, and hammers went missing while they worked on the drapes.

Finally, they were ready for the first day of shooting. The principals for those scenes were driven to the office, and scenes were shot until five o'clock the following morning. The subject of those scenes consisted of what is called a "walk around." A medium of incredible talent and one of the costars of the program was allowed to cover the area outside the office and then to go through every room in the office. This investigation is filmed by her assistant alone. Her sensitive, receptive mind cannot work in the presence of the film crew with a ton of equipment hovering around her. She makes notes in a small notebook as she moves about while her reactions to faint energies form images and sounds that guide her.

Once she is certain that the place has given her all that there is for her to learn, she ends the investigation. Then, the director sits down with her, and they go over in detail what was discovered and where each discovery was made. Then the director sets up each scene to be shot using the information provided by the medium. The crew would sweep into the area with their ton of equipment while the medium and her assistant waited in another area so as not to interfere. Then they would reenact each discovery. These were edited in with actual film clips of her walk through. An exhausted crew broke down the equipment and called it a day, but only for a few hours. They were back in the office at ten o'clock that same morning.

The director had already set up a call sheet for interviews to be shot at 10:00 AM, with me as the first interviewee. The other costar took over these scenes. His job was to handle the historical version of the hauntings and factual information pertaining to the people involved, both dead and alive. The film company relied heavily on a body of information put together after exhausting research by Huntington Paranormal Investigations and Research. This team has among its members two young ladies who did an amazing amount of research on the events that are on record and which took place in the office and the available facts regarding the people involved in these events. Their work represents highly detailed bits of information gathered from many interviews done by phone with many people here in this area that would impress a college professor of journalism. Some of these people were also filmed for the program and took part in the development of the storyline as it aired. Others were not handled in this way. Their interviews were for corroboration of the statements of others, and some were interviewed with the intention of being part of the program but were edited out. That's showbiz.

When the medium walked through the office that night, what she learned, what she imparted to me, was the beginning of the end of the hauntings of my office. Before arriving that night, she was confronted by a ghost in her hotel room. She told me he was a very charming man. He implored her not to believe the women she would find in the office. He said they were vicious liars. They could not be trusted. She could learn all that she needed to know from him. He told her his name. It was not John as I had thought. He said it was Cyrus Kemp Wall. He was the father of Lavina. He preferred to be called Kemp. He did not like Cyrus. When I learned this, I resolved to refer to him as Cyrus, only Cyrus.

When the medium arrived at the office, she knew a tiny bit about it through her conversation with Cyrus, but she did not know that the home of Lavina had been converted into a dental office until she was inside. When she arrived, it was well into the night, and by the time her car pulled away to take her back to the hotel, the sun was making the eastern sky orange.

When she entered the office, she was immediately aware of two women in the corner near the door. They left as soon as she came in—before she even had time to look at them. She said she could tell that they were extremely afraid. Then she went to the hall and the north-side stairwell. She said she was immediately struck by it. The crew had draped it from ceiling to floor with a big black cloth that kept her from seeing the newsprint. I was told this would throw off her reading of the fabric of the building. She picks up energy from the walls and reads events from the past that way. Then spirits come to her as they learn that she can see them. They corroborate what she learns from the building itself. She could hear Lavina, but Lavina was aloof and would not show herself to the medium right away.

On the landing, the medium experienced extreme pain in her leg and back. Then her side. Then deep inside her abdomen. She said she felt that Lavina's hip area had been broken. Her spine was broken, and she had injury to her internal organs. All this was felt on the landing. The medium followed her intuition and ascended the upper flight of steps to the hall. Once inside the room at the top of the stairwell, the medium was overcome with a deep burning sensation in her throat, as if scalded. The medium knew all this pain was being passed to her from Lavina. Then Lavina allowed the medium to see her only one time. She was lying face down on the landing. She was wearing a white slip. The burning in her throat, the pain in her back and leg slowly ebbed away as did the image of Lavina on the landing. She could not understand what the burning throat meant, but everything else was quite clear to her. A few days later, she would tell me, and finally I would know what took place in the stairwell.

The investigator was busy for several days filming in a number of locations around Huntington. He was piecing together historical information about Lavina and what could be gleaned from public records about her death. The film company had a very unusual situation come up during their efforts to obtain hard evidence to use on the show. They were looking for photographs of all the members of the family. All they could obtain was a photo of Cyrus sitting in a truck. Oddly, that photo was obtained from a relative of his who lived just a few miles down the same street the production company had its headquarters located on. The relative agreed to let the company use the actual photo as a prop on the show. When I was handed the photo to see, I had a very odd feeling. I was holding in my hand the actual image of the once-invisible pest that had infested my office. Now he had a name and a face. As I looked at the picture, I could see a hardened man. The face fit the personality I had been dealing with. Before that, Big Guy was anonymous and free to do as he pleased in my office. I began to formulate a resolve to turn the tables on him if I could find a way.

The film crew set up and broke down their equipment time after time as an exhausting series of scenes were shot in rapid sequence. There was no time to rest. With that many people on the payroll, the production company kept things moving as fast as possible. As it was, thousands of dollars were spent each day of shooting, so time was money. Some interviews were shot in locations away from the office. The rest were shot in the office.

Unfortunately, the traffic on Twentieth Street created considerable problems. The sound technician stopped the proceedings often because of the noise from traffic and from helicopters going to and from a nearby hospital. For some reason, Carey was interviewed by the investigator outside the office under the dogwood tree. She told me the sound man was having fits trying to get a clean recording without background noise, but she and the investigator kept doing retake after retake until they finally had enough footage to splice together a complete interview.

The rigging of the lights and sound system took hours to set up and break down each time a different interview was shot. The air-conditioning had to be turned off. The hot lights and the temperatures outside during the sessions caused temperatures inside to soar. The office was like an oven. Still the crew remained concentrated on their work. I did my best to stay out of the way, yet at the same time, I had to be at hand to answer a myriad of questions they had about technical aspects of the equipment in the operatories and where various events actually occurred. The director then used this information to set up each shot. Actually, in almost every case, the area we shot in was not the correct room in which the event occurred. It was necessary to make changes because of restraints placed on the director by the arrangement of the rooms, and articles that could not be manipulated. I found that my input in these decisions was often helpful in the way their equipment was set up. The young men who did this work were very creative. They adapted the equipment to fit the rooms to satisfy the needs of lighting and sound as required by the director. This work was not easy, yet they never acted as though they were the least bit exasperated by the constant changes they had to make, especially when the director discovered that the concept he had envisioned for a scene would not work, and everything had to be broken down and set up in another way. The interview sessions went on until ten o'clock that night. Everyone was tired, wet with perspiration, and hungry.

My scenes with the investigator started at the front desk. He was to ask me what had been going on in the office and I was to give a brief summary of the activities with the ghosts. At one point, I was to remove from the front desk the log book with all the entries made to that date. As it turned out, he was really interested in the log book. He said he had never seen one that documented haunting incidents like the one we had made. It impressed him as he leafed through it. The sheer volume of the book struck him. He would read pages in between takes for our scenes together. Then the director would call us to our places and tell the investigator to put down the book, and we stood. there looking at each other as the technician held up the clack board and snapped the little thing on top of it to mark for the editor which scene was about to be shot.

It was just like the real movies. Shortly after the director said "Cut!" the investigator was back to reading the book. He told me the entries were very convincing, and how impressed he was that so many people were willing to write down what they saw happen and then sign their entries. "That's amazing. I don't know if I would be willing to do that, and yet here are dozens of people who were willing to step up and witness what they experienced. I am convinced that something has to be going on in the place. That's amazing," he said in his clipped Yankee accent. He kept returning to the book during my time with him. I think that book convinced him that what we saw and heard going on in the office was genuine and not something we were making up. He convinced the director that the book should get into the show. I do not think the investigator knew it, but the research people back in Hollywood had asked for permission to photograph every page of the book so that they could use its entries as part of the information they were amassing for the program. I showed the book to the investigator in the first scene of the program, and he brought it out near the end of the show asking the medium if she had ever seen anything like it before. She replied that she had, but nothing as extensive as the one compiled in my office.

After shooting the front desk scene, the investigator and I were taken to the front bedroom where Lavina had died. The heat up there was really building, but everyone stayed focused. As soon as possible, during every break, the lights were turned off. The investigator had started filming with a sports shirt and jacket. He soon regretted his choice of attire. When he asked if he could "ditch" the coat, the director told him he had to keep it on for continuity. If people on screen appear in different clothing from one scene to another, the audience assumes the scene is taking place at a later time. We are all trained by watching shows on television and at theaters that a change of costume means a change in time, unless the costume is changed while the character is on screen. The poor investigator had to endure one-hundred-degree temperatures and higher while wearing a sport coat drenched with sweat. As we talked between scene changes, he told me he could see that I actually cared for the ghost of the girl. We discussed that observation at length. As we looked at the portrait I had made of her, he said, "You have become like a father figure to her." For the first time, it really sank in that it must be true. Janet was the first to say that to me; in fact, she said it often, but for some reason, I did not see myself in that role. For me it was more of a scientific curiosity. I was driven to understand the physics involved in these things over the years, but I had to admit to the investigator that Janet had been right all along. My emotions had come into the picture. I *had* become a father figure. My purely scientific curiosity had evolved into a caring obsession to help the girl find peace. However, to that date, I had failed to do anything to supply any help for her that I could point to. The investigator had come along at the right time and said the right words in the right way to make something click inside my head. It was true. Janet was right. He had pushed Janet's words to the level of acceptance. This would be the first of several revelations that I would experience during the time spent with the film company.

The film crew took down the equipment in the front room and scrambled to the south-side stairwell, with the director delivering instructions to the several cameramen and the lighting director showing the technicians what would be required to get the desired angles filled in with the light treatment envisioned by the director. Finally, all was ready. Paper towels were handed out, and everyone wiped liberal pools of sweat. The clacker board clacked, and we began. I told him about the voice I had heard telling me to get out. This was one of the few stories set in the actual place where it happened. This scene was shot close in and with long shots. Then everything was changed around, and blocking shots were done. Blocking shots are always used when a conversation is filmed. The speaker has his back to the camera and the listener is facing the camera. The listener is coached by the director to nod, raise his eyes and look up or down, and act as though the speaker is saying something about the situation at hand. Then the camera direction is changed, and the speaker becomes the listener and the listener becomes the speaker. These shots are edited into the scene to give the viewer a more interesting visual experience.

The last scene was shot downstairs in operatory 1. I was to describe the situation in which I thought my assistant was in the adjacent operatory with an x-ray she was developing in operatory 3. As I saw her move, I realized she was a ghost and not my assistant. In reality, I was in operatory 2 at the time I saw the ghost through the x-ray window, and the ghost was in operatory 1. For some reason, the director decided to reverse the scene and have me tell the investigator the story as though I was in operatory 1 when the event took place. It is possible that the lighting equipment used for the scene required a bit more room to cast the light into the room so that the view through the x-ray window would be possible. At any rate, the scene was shot in reverse of the actual event. Logistical consideration had to take precedence over historical accuracy, but the essence of each story depicted in the show was honestly portrayed. There was no alteration of the facts in any way other than in the location of the events. We were not told what to say, only where to stand or sit as we told the investigator what we knew, what we saw, and how we felt. We used our own words. There was no script to follow. The program director did not coach any of us in any way in that respect. The truth of our interviews never suffered from these visual alterations.

With the conclusion of the fourth scene, I was excused from the set and told to stay by my phone in case there was any need for me. My daughter, Carey, was next up. She was told to go outside in front of the office in the grassy area out there under the dogwood tree. Many takes were required for the interview because of the increased noise level. Carey and the investigator were not sure why the director wanted to do the interview out there, but he did, and that was where it was done. This did put delays in the production schedule, which were starting to cause pressure to be applied from the production company headquarters in Hollywood. The crew were several days late before they even arrived in Huntington because of other delays in the schedule that were beyond anyone's control. The extreme heat in the office, the difficulties in setting up the scenes, and the pressure to move along at a faster pace would normally set off a group of people working practically on top of each other around the clock; however, there was never the slightest hint of a short temper anywhere. Everyone stayed focused all the way through the shoot. They amazed me. They were a terrific group of people to work with, and I am glad to have had the opportunity.

Karen arrived at about six o'clock that evening after Carey was finished with her interview. The office was still an oven. She was led up to the snack room where the field producer was working at the table. He wanted to go over the setup with her so that she would know what to expect. He also wanted to see if she was nervous about going before camera. He talked with her and gauged her responses, trying to figure out how she would do once the cameras started. The director wanted to conduct the interview in the actual room where the haunting occurred, operatory 2. There was some noise being made by the crew in that area as they arranged the equipment. For that reason, the field producer decided to move to the front bedroom on the south side of the building. He asked Karen if that was okay with her. She told him it didn't matter to her, except that the front room on that side had always made her uneasy when she worked in the office. The field director decided it would be best to move to the room anyway.

The two went down the hall, past the south stairwell, and he entered the room ahead of her. As he was turning to speak to Karen, the unexpected happened. Karen later told me that when she crossed the threshold of the doorway and stepped into the room something struck her deep in her chest like an electric shock. It spread from her chest outward. Up into her head, down into her abdomen, arms, and finally her legs. All this took about one second. Karen said she bent over, her knees buckled, and she staggered forward and would have gone straight to the floor if the producer had not grabbed her. He took both of her hands and steadied her. He asked her if she was okay, and she answered that she did not know. She thought she might be having a heart attack, but the immediate symptoms of the electrical discharge had passed. Only the shock of it remained. At that moment, the producer noticed that her hands were like two ice cubes. That was when she felt the cold. Her inner core was like ice. There she was in a room that was ninety degrees, and she was freezing. She said she felt like a dead person.

The producer led her to a chair, and the two of them assessed her condition, wondering if an ambulance should be called or not. Karen began to feel really ill. She was not able to think clearly. Then one of the technicians came up the stairs to the front room and told them they were ready downstairs. The producer, who was worried about Karen, asked if she thought she was going to be able to go on with the interview. She thought about it and decided to go ahead with it. She told him to go down the steps ahead of her in case she collapsed on them. The two of them worked their way down the stairwell. Karen was helped to a chair in the waiting room.

The producer went into the operatory where the crew was standing by ready to get started. He told them that Karen had been taken ill in the front room upstairs. The director and the investigator came into the waiting room where the investigator took her hands and immediately exclaimed that they were like ice. "You should have felt my hands up there!" she replied. The director knelt in front of her looking intently and asked if she thought she could go on. She said she would have to lean on the counter, and she would try to get through it. With the help of the investigator, who was very accommodating, she made it with only a few retakes and a few blocking shots.

Karen was asked if she could drive home on her own. She assured them that she seemed to be clearing up and went straight home. She told me that she went straight to bed and did not wake up until noon the next day. When she awoke, she said she felt as though she had been taking some sort of drug. The director later told me that she had them all worried, and that the extreme cold was impossible for her to fake. The office was an oven when it happened to her, and the field producer was with her the whole time. She did not run cold water on her hands or hold them against an air vent since the air-conditioning was not on. Whatever it was, she did not fake it. She was not deceiving them; besides nothing of the incident was used in any way by the director. They stuck to the interview as planned. Neither side gained anything from it, so it would be hard to blame Karen or them for trying to inject a falsehood into the show.

Last on the interview list for that day was Charlotte, who had heard a child whimpering in the north side front bedroom. She stopped cleaning the office and listened as the whimpering grew into outright heartrending sobbing. Charlotte told me she had a great time with the crew and the investigator. That was not hard for me to believe. Charlotte does not meet a stranger, and any joke you tell her will prompt her to give you at least three right back and in quick succession. She was just what the crew needed at the end of a long, hard day. By that time, the sun was down below the horizon, and temperatures had dropped a bit. It was time for the crew to wrap the set and get a well-deserved but very late dinner.

During the following days, the crew moved their operations to several locations around Huntington. They wanted the investigator to interview a member of the Huntington Paranormal Investigations and Research team in Jim's Steak and Spaghetti House, an icon of restaurants in Huntington; however, the shooting schedule could not match up with the times the restaurant would be able to accommodate the crew to set up and spend several hours recording an interview. The location for that interview was moved to Spring Hill Cemetery. Several hours were spent before the interview was a wrap, but the editors in Hollywood cut that scene from the final cut. For me, that was unfortunate, because so much labor had gone into their research. The scene was made available online on the Web site of the production company, but it was not the same as being included in the show.

Sound problems encountered while shooting at the office forced the director to ask his field producer to find a place where they could shoot with a quiet background. He asked me if I knew of such a place. I thought immediately of the family room in our house. It is extremely quiet there and could be dressed to resemble a room in the office without difficulty. Janet was on board with the idea. I brought the field producer up to our home along with his sound technician and lighting director. They walked around in the room mumbling to each other. I was like a kid at a top-secret meeting between his parents; I was present, but not actually there. At length, the verdict was rendered. It would take some doing, but the room would do as a surrogate for the office. They left for their hotel to set up meetings to get technical details ironed out. For these meetings, I was not present.

In a few hours, three vans rolled into the driveway, and the crew began unloading the complex panoply of equipment—reels of wire, big black boxes, stands, sandbags, "brutes" (a type of spotlight), mikes, cameras, mounting rigging, a track for the blocking camera to run along, tape, and countless little fittings. Without hesitation, the crew set upon our family room. Just about everything was removed or moved into some corner where it was not going to be in the way. The lengths of pipe and vertical stands were locked together extending across the ceiling. From these pipes, the lights and mikes would be suspended above us as we sat under them. The little track for one camera was set up along one side of the room, and a carriage was mounted on it with the camera set upon that and screwed tightly down. This camera would run back and forth as it shot the four of us sitting at the table.

The table itself was two card tables that Janet supplied along with folding chairs which were placed facing each other two-by-two. Other folding chairs were set up in a different room for the director, assistants, and a makeup girl. Wires ran from the cameras to monitors in this room. Wires also ran from the sound system to earphones for the director and producer. Items were taken from the office and set up in the background to give the illusion that we were actually there. One item was left in the family room. It was our upright piano. Years ago, we discovered when a piano tuner came to the house that the piano in our family room had once graced the best house of ill repute in Huntington. When the "House" was closed up, the piano was sold at auction to a sweet little old lady who taught piano lessons on it. Our piano tuner told us that the instrument had been painted blue and had silver stars on it. Janet had found some blue paint on the back of the piano when she bought it. It had been stripped and refinished at some point after it was removed from the place where it probably enjoyed a more exciting life.

I had not seen the medium at all during the five days the crew had been in our area. Once all the paraphernalia had been put into place and tested to the satisfaction of the director, a call was made to the hotel, and the two stars of the show arrived separately in large sedans. At about the same time, the crew turned on three brutes that were set up on stands in our front yard and shining into the family room through a large window.

Janet had been consigned to our bedroom and told to stay there during the shoot because her footfalls would be picked up by the sensitive sound system. The medium and the investigator did not know that Janet was in a room just a few feet down the hall from them. She later told me that she could hear them exchanging pleasantries as two people do when they are catching up with each other's activities after an absence of several weeks. This verified the statements made by them during the introduction portion of each episode that they do not share information. That was for the both of us an indication that the producers and directors of the show had no intention to deceive their audience.

During that time, I was using our sunroom as my "green room." The field producer came out and told me how he suspected the session would go, and that I should let the medium and the investigator control the tempo of the session. I was not to jump ahead of them with my comments because if I did, the order of the reveal would be disrupted.

Karen was called as the fourth person at the table. Carey was considered, but since she is my daughter, she might be perceived by the audience as a plant or a shill who would enhance deception. Karen would be more neutral. When she arrived, she was given the same instructions. I got the feeling that during one of the previous program tapings, one of the subjects of a haunting had tried to jump ahead of the format, making it difficult for the editors to splice together a reveal that progressed in a logical sequence leading to a properly laid out conclusion. I could see how that could cause a problem for the director, producers, and editors.

She said that she was told that Carey was to be at the reveal, but the executives in the home office in Hollywood had overridden that choice. I did not know that until the day the reveal was shot, and Karen and I only met up moments before we were called to the set. She approached me with a concerned look on her face. She told me that she felt really bad about being asked to replace Carey at the last minute. She also said that she was still experiencing "a little goofy-feeling from the—whatever it was—that hit me at the office." She said she was having trouble concentrating. We were then told that it was time. We went downstairs and took our places at the tables that were butted together and covered with a large piece of black cloth.

Figure 13: The twin house adjacent to 1125 and 1127. The side door can be seen midway between two windows. The same door located at 1125 would have been the door through which Cyrus Wall entered and made his exit on the night of October 19, 1929. The twin house was torn down to make way for Gladwell Pharmacy.

27

The Reveal and a New Task

The reveal was something I will never forget as long as I live. I really hadn't expected any surprises, since I assumed that I knew more about the hauntings than either the investigator or the medium. I did not think there was anything she could learn in such a short time that so many others had not picked up on over years of investigations. I had made up my mind that I would just sit there and act surprised when she told me that there were several spirits in my office. What else was there to say? I assumed she would tell me to call a priest and have the place cleansed of all paranormal activity, and that would be that.

The investigator complimented me on my green polo shirt. I just grinned and thanked him. I chose the shirt for one reason. The contracts and releases I signed before anything could happen in the way of a film crew arriving here to shoot were very specific in the details of what could and could not be done. One "no-no" was clothing that

201

showed any business or sporting logos. I decided to wear the green shirt and my Marshall University class ring at the reveal. I flashed the ring as often as I could with its green stone. I do not know if anyone saw it or not, but I wanted to support my school in spite of the warnings. It worked. I was not sent to my closet for a change of wardrobe. The medium noticed the class ring and, between takes, mentioned it. I removed the ring and handed it to her. She studied it very intently. She really liked the green stone. The investigator became interested in it as well, and when she handed it to him he asked if the class ring was from the local school here in Huntington, Marshall University. I told him it was.

"Oh, I get it, that's the reason for the green polo shirt," he said.

"Yep," I said with a wry smile. He caught my drift, and when I saw the look of understanding on his face, I added, "And there are no school symbols on the shirt, so it's okay, right?"

"No problem here," he answered with a grin.

As the crew stopped the progress of the reveal so that changes could be made in camera angles, or lighting, I had a few minutes to reflect on the information I had received to that point. It had been building pretty much as I had anticipated. But then the mounting evidence the investigator presented took a subtle turn when he divulged the lack of clear evidence explaining the cause of death in the case of Lavina Wall. He turned the discussion over to the medium. In just a few minutes, she revealed more about the hauntings in my office than I had learned on my own in over forty years! It was very clear to me that I had underestimated the medium. Her level of acuity was astounding. I had no idea what she had in store for me. She broke it down for Karen and me, step by step, at first telling us nothing we didn't already know; however, as she got deeper and deeper into her findings, the information she laid out left my knowledge in the dust.

She told Karen and me that when she arrived at the office, she was met by the spirit that had visited her at her hotel several days before. He was now very angry with her for coming to the office. He was very forceful in his attempts to keep the medium from entering the building. When he saw she was going in anyway, he admonished her to reject anything the two women inside the office would tell her about him. He told her that they were evil liars. They would twist the truth about him as would two witches casting a spell. The medium began to see a different side to the charming gentleman ghost that appeared to her at the hotel. She could plainly see the evil in him. She knew he was the one with something to hide; something the two women would reveal to her once she entered and found the stairwell.

While we were between takes, the medium told me that the director had asked her to explain the sensation she picked up on as she went around the outside of the office. While between the building that had been the pharmacy and my office, she felt energy from within that building, now a hair salon. That energy was an expression of death that had occurred in the former structure—the house Mr. Dozier had torn down. The medium sensed a child drowning in a bathtub. The director thought the drowning had occurred in my duplex, not the one beside it, so he wanted the medium to be certain about the correct place in

203

which the child had died. All this was caused by information I had given the director and several producers about a drowning of an infant in a bathtub. I had originally been told that the drowning had occurred in my building.

The Huntington Paranormal Investigations and Research team cleared up my error with their research. The director cleared up the error further when he asked the medium specific details of the death. She was certain it happened in the building beside mine. The director told me he had not discussed this at all with the medium until after she had gone over her findings with him, so she was verifying information he had in his possession for several weeks prior to their arrival to the office. He told me he was amazed by her. None of this made it into the program since it did not involve either my office building or the principal story of Lavina's family. The medium said she placed her hands on the block wall of the building, and at that moment, she saw the child in water face down.

After walking around the outside of the office, the medium stepped inside, entering through the door that leads directly into the waiting room. The door used by patients takes one through an airlock and into the business office. This was the room in which I first met Mrs. Bowen over forty years before. I do not know why the director wanted her to use the door that no one ever uses. It is basically an emergency exit, currently. Only the medium and her assistant entered at that time. The film crew were outside. This examination by the two of them took several hours. The medium picks up on past events and sees spirits that choose to come to her. This is referred to as channeling. Some communication is verbal in nature, but at other times, the spirits let her feel inside her body what physical damage they were subjected to. This takes a toll on her.

A small girl spirit that the medium channels through establishes all these contacts with other spirits. The girl expresses her presence through the medium as the medium gives up herself to allow her transformation to take place. As a result of the transformation, the personality of the little girl comes through and exhibits herself in the physical body of the medium. This shift can be seen as the medium looks and talks like a little girl. Her facial expressions are not hers but those of the little girl. I have heard people remark that the medium is just faking the channeling process; however, I have seen her do this in person. When the little girl comes into her body and the medium speaks through her, the skin on the medium's face becomes very smooth. When the process ends, her face becomes her own, and small wrinkles, the ones we all have as adults, return to her skin. That is not something any grown woman can do at will.

One other fact that caused me to accept the veracity of the medium is that I have kept several secrets about the story of the hauntings from everyone. To this day, not all the secrets have been revealed. That way I can evaluate people who claim to be psychic and try to tell me what they know of my ghosts. This medium learned one of my major secrets. This secret was withheld from even my office staff. The secret was that there had been a door to the outside at the foot of each stairwell on both sides of the building. Either inside or outside of the office, there is no evidence of the doors having been there. The medium found them. This was not shown on the program. Members of the film crew told me that she put her hands on the wall and said, "There once was a door here. It led to the outside." The film crew were amazed when I told them she was right. There was no research that would uncover that fact.

As the night went into early morning, the reveal went on. Scenes were shot hour after hour. We all did our best not to waste time with mistakes as we talked to one another during the taping. Sometimes, the director would stop and ask us to repeat what was just said but in a different way. At other times, a camera angle or a light did not work in the scene. He would ask us to

repeat what was said verbatim after the crew made the necessary changes.

There had been several setbacks, unavoidable ones, that had put the entire project behind schedule. The cast and crew were under a lot of pressure to get the job done in as little time as possible. Time is money. With twenty people punching the clock, the time factor becomes a serious one. I marveled again at the young people who made up the crew. They were focused, dedicated, hardworking professionals all through the time Janet and I were with them.

The medium continued putting together her series of observations for us. I knew that the ghost we called Big Guy was most likely Cyrus Wall. The medium confirmed this point. Then she told me the one thing that opened up the whole story to me. This was revealed to her by Lavina. Her own father was the one who had caused her suffering and death. Her father lifted her up and threw her from the upper hallway over the railing, down to the newel post at the landing, and then onto the landing itself. When she hit the top of the post, her back was broken, and internal injuries were sustained. Her limp body lay on the landing in a twisted pile. She was unconscious for a while. Lavina showed the medium how she lay there. Her face was turned away from the medium for the most part. Her legs were twisted around the post with her feet up against the wall near the uppermost step of the lower flight of stairs. The medium told me that she heard the voice of Lavina but only saw her that one time. Lavina told her that when she regained consciousness, she heard her father sneeringly laugh at her. He said over and over that she was no good.

Then the father turned to the closed door at the end of the hall. He forced his way through that door. Finding the room empty, he found his way through the door to the back room. There he assailed Bernice, Lavina's mother. Then he turned and made his way through the two rooms, slamming both doors as he crossed through them. Down the hall, he stumbled in a drunken rage. He glanced into the front bedroom, perhaps looking for money, and slammed that door. Finally he began to stumble down the stairs toward his daughter who was unable to move. He did not just step over her and descend the final flight. No, he kicked and stomped her immobile body first. Then with his drunken rage abated, he stomped down the lower flight and barged through the door at the foot of the steps. As quickly as that, he was gone from the house.

For a moment, all was still. Then Lavina cried out. Her mother rushed from the back room and found her broken little body on the landing. The suffering she endured during what remained of her life would extend into her afterlife for decades to come.

Now Big Guy had a name and an identity he had managed to keep hidden since October of 1929. He was a killer, and now everyone would know. This was what he had managed to conceal in life and had tried to cover up in death. Maintaining a "good name" was all-consuming for Cyrus K. Wall. That was the one thing he wanted above all else, but his insane hatred for women fired by drunken rage brought him to kill his daughter and his reputation. The ghost of Lavina finally managed to reveal what happened on that night. The secret was out. That was what she had tried to get me to understand all along.

A sketch artist worked with the medium to produce two drawings based on what the medium told her. What they came up with were two amazing works of art. I was extremely impressed by the talent the artist possessed. As I was handed the two drawings during the reveal, I was struck by the face of Cyrus. As soon as I saw it, I felt that I was looking straight at the ghost for the first time. I had seen his photo taken later in life, but the sketch was how I would have expected his ghost to look while he was there on the stairwell.

The investigator produced the painting I had made of Lavina and asked the medium if she thought the girl in the picture could be the same person who had been thrown down the stairs. She looked very carefully at the face. She reiterated that Lavina had not shown herself to any extent while they were communicating. I saw in her expression the recognition of the face in the painting as if she was seeing Livy for the first time. Her reaction might have been the same as when I saw the sketch of Cyrus. "Yes, that is probably what she looked like," the medium answered.

She asked me what the aura of grayish haze meant that I painted Livy in. I told her how I saw Livy in that haze, and in the lighter swirl of fog that encircled Livy as she stood at the top of the stairs. She told me that she sees that same fog-like haze often when things appear to her. She looked at the painting a long time. I had no idea what she was thinking. She seemed to be back on that stairwell with Livy.

The production company was unable to produce any photos of Lavina or her mother. The same stumbling block had vexed the Huntington Paranormal Investigations and Research team; they were the first to obtain a copy of Cyrus Wall in his truck, however.

The pain in Livy's throat had been experienced by two mediums while in the front bedroom where Livy had died. Neither of them could understand what this sensation meant. The investigator stepped in and explained that during prohibition, cyanide was put into alcohol to prevent its use as a drink. This would burn one's throat if consumed. The same conclusion had been reached by the Huntington Paranormal Investigations and Research group, but in a different way. Several of them had experienced a strong scent of peach perfume. Peach pits are a source of cyanide. This may have been a coincidence, but for both mediums and a group of researchers to arrive at the conclusion that Livy may have been given alcohol denatured with cyanide is simply amazing. Leota even expressed that the pain in her throat was not caused by smoke inhalation as I had suggested. She did not know what it was, but she did know what it was not.

The medium carried a small notebook on her walkthrough. She always used a notebook to jot down her impressions when she went to a haunted place. She used this notebook as a general guide for the reveal. After the completion of all the scenes, the medium took out her notebook and began writing instructions for me. The instructions involved a ritual that I was to follow in order to rid the place of Cyrus. After that, I was to have a talk with Livy. I was to tell her that when she was ready to leave the building she could do it now that her reason for staying had been resolved. I was told that eventually she would leave. She would choose the time.

The ritual she wrote in the notebook pages was given to me. She also had a warning. She said that Cyrus might vent his pent-up anger at me during the ritual. I would have to be very careful on both stairwells. That would be where he would most likely try something, like tripping me so that I would fall down the stairs. During the reveal, she presented me with the elements I was to use during the ritual. It would extend over many days. The intent was to get Cyrus out and to prevent him from returning.

I remember the investigator sitting at the table listening to the instructions. He looked at me and said, "This is nuts! She never told anyone to do anything like this before!" He looked at me in disbelief. He later asked me if I really intended to do that. I answered that I didn't see any alternative. He said again that she had never said anything like that before. The medium then told me that the reason she knew I could do it was because she knew that I was a sensitive. That gave me the ability to actually get rid of Cyrus. That was the reason Livy had tried to get her message across to me. She also said that with some years of intensive training I might actually become a medium. I decided to pass on that. Ignorance can be a good thing sometimes.

The crew broke down the equipment and began to replace the items in the room that had been removed. By 3:30 AM, they were just about ready to pull out. Two sedans pulled into our circle alongside the three vans that were packed with the crew and the equipment. Janet came out of her room and joined us on the lawn in front of our house. Karen, the medium, the inspector, the assistant, the director, and the field producer were all standing with me discussing the show. Now that everything was out in the open and the scenes were "in the can," everyone seemed to be relaxed and able to enjoy the moment. Janet asked the medium if she saw any other ghosts during her walk. She said that there were two women in the waiting room who quickly left when she came in, but no other spirits presented themselves other than Lavina and Cyrus. Janet mentioned Paco, but the medium said he stayed away, as did all the others. We assumed that the onslaught of twenty people with equipment that filled nearly every room created enough chaos that the ghosts hid away until it was over. The crew did tell us that at first the ghosts were indeed in the place. They drained batteries, turned lights on and off, and hid tools from the crew as they tried to get their assigned tasks completed on schedule. Paco had been busy.

The vans with the young people in them sped away quickly. As the two sedans were about to pull away, I approached the one with the medium seated in the back seat. She saw me headed toward her and lowered her window. I stepped up to the car and thanked her for all the help she had given me. She said, "I hope you will carry through with my instructions." I assured her that I would. She smiled and said, "Great!" The two sedans pulled away and quietly vanished from sight.

28

The Showdown

For several days after the film crew left us, Janet and I could not talk about anything but what we had just been through. It was some time before I settled down from the excitement enough to concentrate on the task of getting rid of Cyrus. I had never done anything like this before and probably would never again, so I decided I would only have one shot at it, and I had better do it right. The warning the medium gave me kept coming back to me. I did not want to trip on either stairwell. Then I thought of fire. Could Cyrus ignite something? What if he could set fire to the instructions that I would use during the ritual? Just in case such an outlandish possibility was indeed real, I copied the instructions onto aluminum foil. That eliminated the threat of paper catching on fire in my hands.

The thing that required the highest level of preparation was me. I needed the right approach, the right attitude. The ritual had to be the real thing for me, as real as any procedure could be. I convinced myself that neither the elements used nor the words spoken would have any effect without sincere intent behind them. That took time, so it was not until after several weeks of preparation that my mind was clear and receptive enough to actually do what I had to do.

I had gone over the ritual many times, but in order to be certain of going through with it in spite of anything Cyrus had in store for me, I thought I would read from my aluminum page. I recalled the time our little dog, Candy, had backed down the stairs as she looked at Cyrus on the landing. I descended the stairs, crossed the landing, and made it down the lower flight of steps without incident. That was the way I would do it. The only difference was that this time I was kicking Cyrus out for good. He might not like that.

I lit the frankincense at the end of my workday, June 21, 2012. Everyone had left the office, and Janet was just entering. She wanted to wait in the waiting room, just in case. I was at the railing at the top of the stairwell. In a loud voice, I said his name and told him he would have to leave the place and never return. The smoke from the frankincense filled the space of the stairwell in much the same way as did that strange darkness had filled the stairwell the first time I saw Lavina. The ritual had begun. I looked around for any sign of Cyrus. I could not determine if he was there or not, but I decided to continue as if I could see him there with me. I called out his name three times and repeated that he must leave and never return. Only light, peace, and love would be allowed to remain. I picked up the vial of holy water and descended the stairwell while sprinkling it on each step. Then I went into each room and used the vial in those areas. While doing this, I recited the Lord's Prayer. This was followed by the crystals of black salt in all areas of each room, and across each doorway, including the ones closed off. When the doors were opened, the salt was swept out, and the broom was discarded outside in my dumpster.

This procedure was repeated day after day, until I could feel a change. This part is hard to explain, but there was a palpable alteration in the way the office looked and felt. It seemed to be lighter, as if windows were opened on a warm, sunny day. The pall of sadness was lifted. The feeling I had experienced on that first day inside the office was gone. One could say that this was the product of my imagination. While I admit to having an active imagination since childhood, I know the difference between the imagined and the real. This was real.

Shortly after the ritual was completed, a patient asked me if I had painted the office recently. I said no, the office had not been painted and then asked why she had asked that. She told me the office was lighter and brighter. She was certain the walls were a lighter shade. I told her we had done something, but painting was not it. She would not drop the subject with a silly answer like the one I gave her. So I sat down and gave her a thumbnail sketch of the history of the place. The fact that she saw a change without knowing anything about what had been going on was not lost on her. She was impressed with herself, and so was I. I told her she was a sensitive who did not know it until that day. Now she is reading spiritual subjects and finding her own way through this maze of the paranormal. What she picked up on was what my employees and I saw. The mood of the building had changed. The pall of sadness was lifted.

29

The Light Behind the Clock

The medium told me that I would know when it was time to start helping Lavina leave the office. She told me to have quiet talks with her. I was to assure her that somewhere in the office, there would be a bright area. That area of light would be her passageway to peace. Only she could find the place. Only she could decide when it was time. I felt like a father having talks with his daughter about her wedding and the new chapter her life would soon be starting. Only this daughter remained unseen. It was a bittersweet time, an end that involved a beginning. So it was with Livy and me. We had been through so much together, and yet there was still so much left unsaid. There were still so many things that I didn't know about her that I wanted to learn.

There was one possibility for me to find out what Livy was doing now that Cyrus was out of her way. Was she happy? Leota was my one and only hope to communicate with her. Through Leota, I would be able to find out what was going on.

Leota returned to find everything changed. With the expulsion of her tormentor and the truth of her cause of death exposed, Livy was changed. No longer the shy, sad little girl, Livy had become a much younger child in a white dress with a lace-bordered pinafore and a light-blue bow in her brushed and curly hair. She could not stand still. She ran around Leota in a whirlwind of speed. From room to room, she danced and played catch-me-if-you-can!

Leota told me Livy's transformation was astounding. She greeted Leota with a big smile and sparkling eyes expressing carefree joy. Leota asked Livy where she liked to play, sensing the stairwell had been abandoned as the place she spent her time. With bounding energy, Livy took Leota's hand and led her to the wall in the waiting room near the stairwell. The wall had once had a double window. The window was the one I had noticed when I stepped into the room for the first time. Evidently, Livy jumped through that window, as one expects children to do. In her time, people had open windows in their homes; using windows to exit houses is a lost art in our time. I had to explain the closed off window to Leota who was puzzled by what Livy expected her to do. "I can't go that way, Livy," said Leota.

"Here," I said. "Go out the front door." We went out and found Livy in the space between the office and the building next door, now a hair salon.

Livy could go through the solid block wall and enter the salon. Leota was perplexed until I explained that there had been a house there that had a door just like the one I had closed off at the base of the stairwell. Livy was seeing the house, not the salon that was there now, but the house that was there in about 1920. We suspected Livy had a friend who lived there. That may have been the girl named Sara, who was with Livy when Leota first visited. The two girls may have played together during the times when Cyrus was not in the picture.

Leota asked Livy if she would show us her bedroom. We all went up the stairs to her room as Livy bounded ahead in a flurry. This time, Tim, Leota's husband, recorded the session with a video camera. Once we were gathered in Livy's bedroom, Leota placed a small recording device and some papers on a table near Livy's closet door. We placed some billiard balls on the billiard table, which stands in the middle of the room. We thought Livy might be enticed to move one of the balls, but instead she whirled under and around the table in a frenzy of activity that was of no apparent purpose other than as an expression of her extreme joy. When asked if she wanted to play with Leota's hair again, there was no answer. Instead she raced around the billiard table and made for the door. Leota snapped a photo of Livy as she reached the door. The print shows an orb beside her husband who was near the open doorway. "Well, she just left," said Leota. Livy was exhibiting a level of energy none of us expected. She could not stay in one place and had little interest in talking with us, especially not about any serious subjects.

We walked along the hallway, through the long room, and into the back room. Leota wanted to try to connect with the lady who spoke French, but she was not willing to communicate with us at all. Then in popped Livy, our little ghostly tornado. She grabbed Leota's hand and pulled her back to the stairwell. Leota sat down on the top step and asked Livy if she would say her name. "Downstairs!" was all she would say. We all followed as Livy led Leota down, through the waiting room, out the front door, and back into the space between the office and the hair salon.

I noticed Leota stopped and faced the salon at the exact spot across from the area where my side door once opened. Livy was once again inside the house that once stood there. She was trying to get Leota to shift time and enter the house with her. Livy turned around and came back to the open doorway of the house. She seemed to be unable to grasp the fact that to us, it was a solid block wall. Leota tried her best to make Livy understand that we could not see the house she was in. We could only see the building that replaced it.

This apparent ease with which spirits seem to be able to shift time as one unbroken spectrum could open avenues of awareness from which we could benefit. The only task for us would be to find a way to communicate with the residents of that realm. If we could do that, we would open the very heart of knowledge we can only imagine now. Livy and other spirits seem reluctant to allow us to do this. Perhaps they will not open up to us because they are aware that we are not ready for the information we would have made known to us... Will we have the answers once we are on the other side, or will there be secrets that will always remain? After all, just because they are on the other side does not mean that they have any greater understanding than we do on this side of the death experience.

Livy finally emerged from within the salon and started running circles around Leota as she stood on the walk between the buildings. Leota finally convinced our little whirlwind to return to the office, but she would not go back in until she had crawled through an opening in the block foundation that once supported the front porch floor. As with the house next door, this block foundation did not exist in our time, only Livy's. She laughed and winked at Leota from this hiding place. Leota could not see the entire scene, only the foundation of the porch with the opening. She was perplexed by what she saw. I explained that the foundation and front porch were all removed after I bought the place. Here, again, Livy was pushing back the clock. Leota never could see the entire setting anywhere Livy took her. She could only see the immediate surroundings around Livy. We do not think that Livy understood this.

Once we did manage to get Livy back inside the office, we decided we would try to have a serious conversation with her. I wanted to do that while I had Leota present so that I could make certain the message was getting through. I asked Livy if she could see anywhere in the office a place she could go through into where there was bright light. I suggested that she might be able to see her mother there and other members of her family. Livy asked if such a place could be behind something. With a nod of Leota's head, I answered that it could. To this, she answered that there was such a place behind the large grandfather clock that stood on the landing in the stairwell, but she said that she was reluctant to get close to it. Leota sensed that she was afraid of the area, so she stepped into the conversation and told Livy that if she would only look into the area of light, she would see a wonderful place where she could be even happier than she was right now.

Leota told me that Livy was still hesitant, and so I said that we did not want her to do anything if she was not ready yet. There was a spark of interest produced by our urging that Leota sensed. And she said she thought Livy was about to enter the area. Then she asked Leota if she could come back and visit. Leota was caught off guard. She hesitated and then told Livy she was not certain she would be able to return. At this point in the conversation we were standing at the first step of the stairwell. We all heard Livy's little feet scamper up the stairwell and out of our area. "Well, that's that," Leota said.

Our efforts had come so close, but we were a little shy of convincing Livy to enter the portal. We felt we had come a long way with her, but she needed more time before she would be ready to try this new phase of her existence. For now, she was enjoying the complete freedom to just be a little girl without fear or pain. I could understand her point of view. Leota and I decided it would be best if we backed away from the subject for the time being. At least we knew she had found the portal and understood that it was nothing to be afraid of. We marveled at the fact that the portal would be on the landing of the stairwell. Could that have some significance? We had no idea. It was best just to let her play with her little friend in the house next door.

The only direct evidence I had of this wild encounter with Livy was the unmistakable sound of her little feet on the stairs as she scampered away from us and entered her bedroom. We assumed she had tucked herself away inside the closet. That was the last time I had any direct contact with Livy in which her presence was perceived through my own senses. As I reflected on that moment we shared, I decided it was appropriate that it occurred in the stairwell, where it had all begun.

The following evening, the four of us met at our home to review the video Tim had taken at various times during our wild romp with Livy. The session in the front bedroom was recorded while Leota was asking Livy if she would like to move the billiard balls on the table or play with her hair as she had done before (so that we would be able to see it on the film later). During the session, we were all watching the billiard balls, but Livy played a trick on us. The small recorder Leota had left on the table was behind her. It began to rotate as it lay on the table. At the same time, the folded papers lying on the table beside the recorder began to move in a very strange way. The pages began to move up and down rapidly. The only way one could replicate what the folded pages were doing would have been to hold them down at the folded end and force a blast of air on the edges of the pages opposite from the folded side. The air would cause the pages to fluctuate up and down, while the pages would not be allowed to scoot away from the source of the compressed air.

As these objects stopped moving, we could see a shadowy form moving away from the area where the recorder and folded papers were lying and passing behind Leota and the billiard table to the left of the screen out of the camera's view. None of us noticed either the rotating recorder, or the flapping papers, to say nothing of the shadow that passed between Leota and the curtains behind her. We were focused on the billiard balls, hoping to see them move a little. A little joke had been played on us.

Then we played back the recorder Leota had used during her visit. While Leota was outside between the two buildings, and Livy was trying to get her to walk through a solid block wall and join her inside, we all heard Livy produce a squeal-like laugh. It was the sound of a little girl having the time of her life. At the end of the recording, we could hear Livy's footfalls as she scampered up the stairwell and away from us.

These revelations convinced me that Livy was not ready to leave. Clearly, it was best for us all to back away and let this happy child enjoy her time in the building and in the house next door. We were surprised to see her as a much younger little girl than anyone had seen any time prior to that session. She moved backward in her life so that she could find the point where she had enjoyed a moment of carefree play with a little friend next door. Who was I to suggest that she should stop all that and leave the place? I decided I should leave well enough alone and let her do all she needed to do in her own way and in her own time. I finally learned how little time means to those on the other side. By that point, I had essentially pulled away from her. She was in charge now.

Figure 14: The long room, on the second floor, with the carousel horse, where Livy said, "I'm not a horse!"

30

More Shenanigans...Then...Quiet

On August 1, 2012, a new assistant in the office was working with me on a patient. Suddenly she turned around, saying something as she turned. I noticed her but thought no more of it. We continued the appointment and excused the patient, who left the operatory and headed for the front desk. As I was writing notations on the patient's chart, the assistant told me that she had been certain that Morgan had entered the room and tapped her on the back to get her attention. That was when she turned around. She assumed Morgan was going to tell her that she had a call out at the front desk. That was a logical assumption, since it does happen from time to time. When the assistant realized that Morgan was not standing behind her, she knew it had been one of the ghosts. I, on the other hand, was unaware of anything entering the room or standing behind the assistant. There was nothing that I could recall that had indicated to me the presence of a ghost in the room, but that in itself is not unusual. At times there is no visible change in the space around a ghost, while at other times, there are drops in temperature and a change in the level of light. I have always wondered why that is so.

On August 20, 2012, a paranormal investigation was conducted in the office with limited results. One female investigator on the team wrote in our log book that she had heard the squeal of a child coming from one of the rooms in the back of the office and noticed the smell of a sweet floral-like scent in another room. Another investigator in that group wrote that his K-2 device recorded maximum swings in electrical fields several times in several rooms. He wrote that the intensity of the device as it reacted to some unseen electromagnetic field that moved through the rooms was impressive. He had never experienced such high levels with his equipment.

Not long after that, our hygienist, Julie, saw what she recognized as the spirit of one of our patients who had recently died. He was standing at the front desk, looking at her. She knew immediately who he was. He was wearing a white shirt with blue stripes. I am certain that our patient was wearing that shirt the last time he was in the office. This makes me wonder about the theory that portals open and spirits either come into our world or leave by way of them. That might explain why the ghost of a patient would show up at our front desk during office hours. We never saw him again, but his ghost is an example of the many we have experienced in the office that are without much of a connection to the place. Obviously, they did not all die in the office, so they can come to the office without their deaths being the means by which they enter. Perhaps there are more portals than the one Livy found in the stairwell. That portal might have been for her alone. The patient Julie saw grew up in the neighborhood near the building. Perhaps he entered the building through a portal somewhere inside the place and made his way to his old neighborhood. I like to think that is what happened.

Ghosts can be amusing in the things they do, and by the way, they affect those of us on this side of the equation. During Thanksgiving weekend in 2012, a young couple was given a tour of the office. They had heard about the hauntings, and they asked if they could see the place during their visit to Huntington. The date and time were arranged, and I met them in the parking lot to begin their tour.

As we entered the office, I asked if they had any means of sound recording. The young man produced his cell phone and said he could set it to record. "Good, turn it on, and let's see if we can catch a ghost saying something," I said.

The wife said, "Do you actually mean that?" I told them their chances of recording a voice are higher than their chances of not getting anything. The fellow quickly set his phone to record. It had not occurred to either of them that they could record the voice of a ghost!

I showed them my EMF monitor and explained the theory behind the use of the EMF meter for the detection of ghosts. When I turned it on, it went ballistic, immediately. As I moved it around, it was soon apparent that Livy was standing right in front of the wife.

"She likes you," I said. As I moved the monitor from the floor up to about five feet from the floor the meter stopped. "That is how tall Lavina is." Moving side to side,

227

they could see how slender she was. It was easy to render this conclusion. All I had to do was to move the meter up and down, and side to side. The two had a perfect demonstration of how the EMF worked at locating a ghost. The wife had long dark hair, dark-brown eyes, and a deep complexion. She could have been Livy's sister. When I told the young woman this, she was a bit shaken. "This will be a good night." The two gals were already a pair, and we were still in the outer office. From there we went into the waiting room. The carousel horse from Camden Park was a hit with the wife. She loved carousel horses, and so did Livy. The EMF found Livy sitting on it. Then she went to one of the waiting room chairs. From there, she zipped away into the stairwell. We toured the two operatories and then ascended the stairs past the portrait, which we looked at for a time, and then to the railing at the top of the stairs. I described the father picking Livy up and throwing her down to the landing from there. Then the description of the ten days spent in the front bedroom, ending in Livy's death.

Quietly we walked down the hallway and into the long room. "Oh look! There's another carousel horse!" exclaimed the wife. I showed her this second horse that was used in the production *Carousel* in the amphitheater in Ritter Park. We turned to the back room on the north side, the snack room, and the front room on the south side, and down the south stairs. We returned to the waiting room where I gave the pair a chance to ask any questions they might have. The husband noticed a book among my collection of reading materials. It was one of the histories of Marshall University. He said, "I have seen that book

228

before. My aunt is pictured in it." Then he picked up the book, thumbed through it, and found the picture, showing a group of Marshall coeds lined up along a railing. He pointed out the lady who was his aunt and told me that she had been a nurse in the Pacific Theater during World War II. After that, we exchanged some pleasantries and left the office.

The following day, the husband called me. His voice was full of excitement to the extent that he could not contain himself. On his cell phone recording were three electronic voice prints. He was ecstatic. He described each recording and then let me hear each one over the phone. The first one was Livy. Clear as could be, she had replied when the wife said, "Oh look! There's another carousel horse!" Livy, who was sitting on the horse, said, "*I'm* not a horse!" Hearing this made a chill go up the fellow's spine. He played it for his wife, and she couldn't believe her ears. They played it over and over. Then they advanced through the recording to the point at which the husband told me about his aunt working as a nurse in the Pacific. At that point, a rough voice interjected, "Japs!" Then, as we were about to leave, a recorded voice said, "I am Lewis, and this is Carmella." The voice was of a middle-aged man, very pleasant, and aware that he was talking to us. This is because the young man held the recording phone up close to his chest nearly the entire visit, taking it away only to show me the photo of his aunt in the book. The speaker, Lewis, had to be fairly close to the husband and in front of him. Judging from my own voice as it was recorded during the tour, I was most clear when facing the phone and standing close to and in front of it. Lewis was standing in front of the young man when he manipulated the phone to record his voice.

The young couple had entered the office expecting nothing more than a tour of the place. As it turned out, they left with three of the best recordings ever made in the office. Any paranormal investigator would drool over them. The loud, crisp, and clear quality of the voices was unmatched. Beginner's luck? Perhaps.

On December 8, 2012, another paranormal group set up their equipment and spent the night learning about the haunted dental office. They had a very active night with many responses to their questions from a number of different ghosts. One of the favorite entities that often communicated with younger patients was the incomparable Paco. On this night, he interacted with several investigators, and everyone had a really good time.

One investigator reported seeing the black shadow that so many others had seen crossing the room time after time. I believe this is a residual haunting. This is some form of energy that is repeating an event over and over. There has been no communication between a residual and a living person that I know of. Since it has nothing to do with the rantings of Cyrus, or the playful antics of Livy, it will most likely remain in the area doing what it does. I will have to find out if I am right someday.

In this general area, the *other* black shadow *does* interact with people. It is not the same as the shadow that crosses the room. This other black thing seems to be shy. It flees the area when people see it. One of the investigators on this particular team spotted this other black thing in the back room on the north side, where I have seen it. This thing can move really fast. In a blink, it can cross the room and be gone. No one has been able to figure it out.

On January 8, 2013, Becky smelled cigar smoke again. She stopped in her tracks and tried to see if she could figure out just where the smell was coming from. As she was trying to figure out just where the highest density of the cigar smell was, it began to dissipate. Then it was gone completely.

On January 31, 2013, I was making my rounds in the office turning off lights and equipment. I was the only one left in the place. Everyone else had been gone for half an hour. I was in the waiting room when I heard a sound that seemed to come from either operatory 1 or operatory 2. It sounded like something had fallen out of a cabinet and after bouncing off the counter, thumped on the floor. Assuming one of the assistants had returned to the office while I was on the second floor, I was walking in the direction of the two operatories asking if she might need help with something. I saw no one in the first room, and the second room was unoccupied as well. As I came back through the two rooms, I turned off the lights and equipment switches to shut down the air compressor and vacuum pumps. I assumed Paco might be playing one of his tricks on me. I thought nothing more about it than that.

As I walked through the hall toward the waiting room, I saw in my peripheral vision a motion up high in the stairwell. I stepped back one step and looked up from the foot of the stairs. I expected to see one of my assistants leaning over the railing, about to tell me why she had returned to the office. I was taken aback by what I saw. The large ceiling light hanging by four chains from the same spot where the lone lightbulb once illuminated the space was swinging in a very wide arc. It was nearly about to strike the walls on each side as it made its way back and forth. Only a very serious earthquake would make that light swing so violently. I stood there watching it in total amazement. What was that all about? Was one of the ghosts trying to send me a message of some kind? Could Cyrus have found a way back in? Was this his way of telling me that he was back?

I decided my best option was to counter this action with one of my own. I ran up the stairs and demanded that whoever caused the light to swing like that to show himself. As I stood there looking around in the upper hall, the light slowly settled down and all became quiet and still. The light had made a creaking sound as it swayed wildly. As it settled down, the creaking noise stopped. I stood there watching. There was no noise and no swinging.

"Livy, honey, if that was you swinging on that light, I apologize for yelling at you. Please don't do that anymore. You might cause the light to fall down." The light was one of two I obtained when the old Orpheum Theater was undergoing a complete renovation. (It was cut down into several smaller theater auditoriums. Back in its heyday, there were six of those lights mounted high overhead. I remember looking up at them and wondering how they changed the lightbulbs.) I stood there for a long time looking around. Nothing else happened, so I went down the stairwell and left the office. I do not have a clue what that was all about. Was it Livy? Was it Paco? I think if Cyrus had reentered the building and started the light swinging, he would not have quit until it broke loose. That would have been a perfect way for him to make the statement that he had returned.

February 13, 2013, was just another day at the office. I unlocked the front door and shut off the alarm system. Then I began making my way through the office turning things off and on as the situation required for each item. There are thirty-six switches in all. My head was clearing itself and ending its ho-hums. I opened the door to the front bedroom closet—we call it Livy's closet—which is where I keep my uniform scrubs. That was when I came fully awake. A chill went up my spine. There in the center of the floor right where I could not possibly miss it was a red foam ball. It had been among the toys that people had left at the top of the stairs for Livy.

Leota had suggested that all the toys should be removed from the top of the stairs and put in this closet, since Livy and her friend Sara seemed to hide there. This ball was often moved around when it was kept with the other toys in the hallway. One paranormal group watched as it rolled down that hall, stopped rolling, and started up again, stopped, and then vibrated as if someone were trying to get it going again. I was there when this occurred. Unfortunately, all cameras had just been packed away. We had no record of the incident. When the medium from the show told me that it would be best to remove the toys, I must have missed this one. How that could have happened is a puzzle. All the toys were kept in one spot on the closet floor. I put the toys in a box and put the box in the back room for a period of time. Then I removed them to our home. All except the red foam ball, apparently.

I asked out loud, "Livy, are you trying to tell me something?" This was a puzzle indeed. Was she telling me that I had missed this one toy, and that she was placing it in the center of the closet floor so that I would find it and take it home to be with the rest of the toys? Or was it something else? Had she and her friend carried the ball away and then brought it back so that I would know that they wanted all the toys back in the closet? Then there was the question of where the red ball had been all that time. For several days, I tried to solve the puzzle and decide what I should do. At last I decided I would stay the course with the advice the medium had given to me. I took the ball out of the closet. Then I sat down in a chair next to the saddle where Livy often sat and told Livy that I was going to take the ball home with me that evening and put it with her other toys. I said that I was not doing this as a means of punishment, for she had done nothing wrong. I had decided that she had placed the ball in the closet as a way of telling me that she wanted me to put it with the rest of the toys. I thought this was her way of telling me that she was through with the toys and didn't want them any longer. I promised that I would keep them safe for her. Now that I have had considerable time to reflect on the incident, I think that Livy had indeed matured past the point that she wanted to play with toys. Perhaps with the absence of her tormenting father, she had at first regressed back into early childhood and played in a cathartic ecstasy; however, with time, she advanced through the joyful childhood she did not have in her lifetime, and through maturation of her personality, transformed gradually into the older girl who came to realize she might finally be ready to pass through that portal.

By this time, Livy seemed to become less active, while a woman, who may have been her mother, became more active. In May of 2013, my assistant, Rachel, was cleaning up operatory 2 at the end of the day. Her husband, Don, had entered the office and was waiting to take her home. I was at the front desk and told him he could go back where Rachel was working if he wanted. He went back to operatory 2 where she was concluding her work, and they engaged in small talk. Suddenly they were drawn to something they both saw in operatory 1. A woman with black, shoulder-length hair and a white dress was standing in the corner of the room as Rachel and her husband looked at her through the x-ray window. They both saw her at the same time. When they entered operatory 1, the room was empty.

Another paranormal investigation encountered the mysterious black shadow in the back room on the second floor. They had several other experiences during the night that they spent in the office which resulted in an animated review written about their time there.

Our cleaning contractor, Stacy, had an experience while working in the office after hours during May of 2013. She, too, saw a woman with black curly hair and a white dress in the operatory where Rachel and Don had seen an apparition. In both instances, the image was solid enough to cause all three people to assume that they were looking at a living person. Upon seeing no one in the room when they quickly turned to get a closer look, the image was gone. Was she trying to convey a message, or was she simply caught at a moment when she was fully materialized? Was she trying to understand what had happened to her dining room? Perhaps she was just as puzzled as all of us.

On July 6, 2013, one of the last groups to investigate the office had invited someone who was not interested in paranormal investigation at all. Nonetheless, they were hoping to get him involved in an indirect way. Since he was a dog trainer, the investigators wanted him to train a dog to act as a sensitive. They had read about how animals of all sorts sometimes responded to paranormal beings, and they wanted to try out their idea. But first, they needed a trained dog, and to have that, they needed a trainer who had some idea of the general concept of a paranormal investigation. So they convinced the trainer to come along and observe them so as to develop a system by which he could train a dog for their use. The trainer was skeptical in all respects but agreed to at least go along with them as an observer.

This set the stage for a bit of scary comedy. Of all people, this poor fellow was singled out to be the target of a very frightening apparition. He was standing in the doorway between the snack room and the long room near the laboratory saloon doors. All lights were out, but there is always some ambient light from the upstairs windows. As our dog trainer watched, a sliver of white that quivered like a shimmering reflection of light on water caught his eye as it drifted toward him. It came closer and closer as he stood there watching. He was trying to figure out what was causing this strange light.

It stopped right in front of him. Then it began to change. It became black and grew to a thickness of about eighteen inches in width and grew to about three feet in height. By this time, it was a dense black mass. He took flight. In his wake were a string of expletives not fit for polite company. When he reached the stairwell, he stopped and gathered himself, somewhat. After all, he was a big macho sort of a guy. He went the rest of the way down the stairs to the waiting room where the other two women were holding an EVP session with a little girl who would not give her name but had been giggling several times on the recording. This giggling was as audible as both women had reported hearing it.

It just so happened that Leota was in the area just after this investigation. With a shift in activity occurring, I thought it would be a good idea to have her come by and get a feel for what was occurring in the office. Happily, she agreed. She noted that there was a difference in the atmosphere. Livy was present but reticent. Leota did not receive much communication from her; she seemed to be in deep thought and not talkative. The medium did lay to rest any concern that Cyrus may have found his way back into the office; his presence was not one that could be hidden if he were there, and she assured us that he was *not* back.

But there *was*, in fact, a male presence there who met Leota as she entered Livy's room. He was a dapper older gentleman whose name was George, and he had grievances! He began to rattle them off to Leota. First, he was annoyed by investigators disturbing his "after office hours" time, during which he considered the upstairs area available to him and a friend to contemplate the chess set near the snack room in the long room. Leota imitated George for me by slicing her hand through the air as she paced the floor, muttering, "Every weekend! Every weekend they're here! Disrespectful! Disrespectful!"

George wanted the investigators to stop coming in, asking the same questions, and asking for favors, such as making EMF meters light up or moving objects. Leota questioned whether recent investigators had been specifically rude or confrontational, as George was particularly fired up and repeated "Disrespectful!" many times. She also asked if there was a different kind of encounter with investigators recently, as George seemed to suggest he had taken care of one situation himself, though he wouldn't disclose *how* he had done so. It does make one wonder about the shimmering light that confronted the recent investigation group. Was that George?

But George wasn't finished with his list of demands. He was also dissatisfied with the music being played in the office. "Symphony," said Leota, on George's behalf. "He wants to hear more symphony and other classical music as well. He's specifically mentioning Mozart and Haydn." Well, that wasn't a huge challenge; I could set our stereo system to any category on the satellite system. Since we seemed to have received all the messages we were going to receive for the night, I decided to extend an olive branch to George. I announced that I would turn the stereo on the classical station and leave it playing all weekend—just for him! I set the station and turned the volume up so it would be audible throughout the office, and we left as the host on the radio was describing the evening's program.

238

As I drove home, I decided to set my car stereo to the classical station and listen to what music George would be hearing at the same time. The announcer was still talking about the program. It must be something very special to have this much introduction; George would be very pleased indeed! I was startled by the sudden crash of chords and the other-worldly melody that emanated from my speakers. What sort of classical music was this? During the next break, I learned that this weekend was a special program on the classical station: Movie Theme Music. Of course, the first song to be played was a sci-fi movie theme. Well, it'll only play for an hour or so; perhaps George would have a sense of humor about it and enjoy the music anyway. I had to contact Leota on Monday, July 8, 2013, and tell her about my good intentions gone wrong. When I arrived at the office, I was greeted by silence—not a note of classical music could be heard. I checked the stereo and saw that the volume had been turned down all the way. I guess George didn't appreciate Movie Theme Night after all. He actually hated it; the stereo never worked correctly after that, and I eventually had to replace it entirely. I had ticked off a ghost—and he let me know it!

On September 26, 2013, while performing a procedure on our last patient of the day, I saw repeatedly a woman with curly black hair and a white dress standing behind Rachel. The apparition was not solid, and it seemed out of focus. There was an aura of atmospheric haze around it, as if it was neither willing nor able to completely materialize. I thought that if I did not react to it I might be able to see it better, but after three or four attempts to materialize, it faded slowly away one last time and did not return. I had the distinct feeling that it was trying to communicate with me. But what was its message?

February 5, 2014, Rachel and I were performing an operation on a patient in the midafternoon. All three of us heard someone walking around in the room above us. I asked them if they heard it, and they both said that they did. "Is that a ghost?" the patient asked.

"Yes, it is," I answered. The very next patient told us that she thought she might have seen a ghost as she approached the office after parking her car in the parking lot. As she made her way toward the back of the office, a motion in the left-side window caught her attention. She looked up at the window and saw a woman move the curtains aside and look at her. The woman dropped the curtains and stepped back from the window. This was occurring at the same time the three of us in operatory 2 below the left side window were discussing the sound of someone walking above our heads. This concurrence of sights and sounds from different perspectives by four people provide, in my mind, very good evidence of a haunting.

On February 8, 2014, a paranormal group arrived to set up their equipment for an investigation. As they were doing this, one young woman pulled me aside and told me she had a message for me. Assuming she meant that she had a message from one of the investigators, I was shocked when she said it was from *Livy*. The young woman described two vivid dreams she had several weeks before the scheduled investigation. Livy came to her in the dreams. She told her to thank me for being the father she never had while she was alive. For me, this was an important communication. I asked the investigator to write in the log what she remembered of her dreams. Eventually the idea hit upon me that her brief recounting was a final message from Livy.

This was her way of saying good-bye.

Paranormal investigations continued throughout the year, turning up less and less evidence of our spiritual residents. We noticed enough change that I again contacted Leota to inquire if she had ever heard of spirits just seeming to disappear from a place they have inhabited for decades. She smiled as she joked about it being nearly All Hallows' Eve and perhaps they were taking their vacation early this year. But then she became serious and asked if I had received any further contact from Livy. She had noticed each time she visited that Livy had a completely different demeanor—first frightened child, then deliriously happy child, then pensive older girl.

It was Leota's impression that Livy had finally been allowed to go, through processes that she had not been able to follow before. After all, how could anyone get over a traumatic experience when the person who caused it was constantly there, harassing and tormenting his prey? She had stayed such a young girl because that was how Cyrus made her feel—small and helpless. She had a lot of catching up to do, and without that negativity around, she could "grow" and process all that had happened to her. Leota suggested that perhaps Livy had finally had all the time she needed to work through her emotions and feelings; perhaps she had "matured" enough to finally move on. And we knew that she knew where to find the passageway.

241

Leota's final question sealed the deal. She asked what Livy's "dates" were—as in what were her birth and death dates on her death certificate. "Maybe there's no connection at all," Leota said, "but I feel like Livy would choose a date that was significant to her as a date to leave."

My chest tightened as I replied, "She died October 29th!"

Our time together had come to an end. I did not figure this out at first. At the time, I assumed she had simply managed to find someone who was receptive to her, and her words did not convey anything beyond that which she said. Then I came to the realization that the office had changed. There was an emptiness that had not been there before. Two recent investigations had resulted in no evidence of paranormal activity of any kind in the office. The residual black thing still seems to linger, but it is so sporadic in its appearances that a series of investigations might never pick up the activity unless one had the good fortune to be at the right place at the right time. My cleaning service last saw the black thing in mid-October of 2014. Whether or not it still inhabits the back room is unknown.

Once I realized that there had been a dynamic shift in the spirit activity, the message Livy had conveyed to me through the young woman took on new meaning. It was her way to get a message to me as directly as she was able. She had found a way to say good-bye to me. As always, I finally managed to misunderstand what should have been obvious. I opened the Ghost Log and read once again the way the young investigator had worded Livy's message. Then I read it over and over. "Good-bye," was what Livy was trying to get me to understand. She was not just thanking me. So that was it. Livy had sent her thoughts to me through the sleeping mind of a woman neither of us knew all that well, but she had chosen the right time and the right place for the message to come through. And there it was. (Sometimes my slowness astounds me.)

In her own quiet way, Livy had left me and the place we both knew so well, the north-side stairwell at 1125 Twentieth Street.

I wonder when the time came for her to leave if she paused and looked around the stairwell one last time before entering the portal on the landing. Or was she finished with that place and did not wish to be there any longer? After Cyrus was kicked out, she reverted to her childhood and, as days passed, matured into a young woman, able to face the next phase of her existence with courage and understanding.

Figure 15: They are gone now. Goodbye Livy, I wish you well.

EPILOGUE

When Livy left the office, the others, who seemed to be a mystery to everyone who experienced them, removed themselves as well. Perhaps they had come into the office to protect Livy and her mother and sister. Once Cyrus was exposed for what he was and was kicked out, Livy could enjoy her life. But first she had to find a moment when she had been happy in the place. From there, she went wild in a rampage of childish fun. During this juncture, her mother and sister were also free to come out of hiding and enjoy the freedom they were unable to have while Cyrus ruled.

Then they left, quietly. Their time here had come to an end. All parties come to an end. The guests leave, and the place once filled with laughter, singing, and loving joy returns to a place of quiet. Only in this case, the party was not one of much laughter and singing. The extent of the discord in the stairwell and adjoining rooms will never be known, I suppose.

All this happened in my office. Some people experienced parts of it, while others experienced none of it. Some still scoff at my tales of haunting, but I understand that.

And so, now, dear reader, you know much about the memories that were going through my head as I stood at the railing in the second-floor hallway in the evening after work, as those amber rays of the setting sun wove their magic around me. Now, as then, all I can think to say is, *"Good-bye, Livy. I wish you well."*

CPSIA information can be obtained
at www.ICGtesting.com
Printed in the USA
LVHW022058140721
692685LV00010B/592